Quilts for Girls and Boys

10 Projects

BARBARA ROBERTS

Martingale
& COMPANY

BOTHELL | WASHINGTON

Credits

President . . . . Nancy J. Martin
CEO . . . . Daniel J. Martin
Publisher . . . . Jane Hamada
Editorial Director . . . . Mary V. Green
Design and Production Manager . . . . Stan Green
Technical Editor . . . . Karen Soltys
Copy Editor . . . . Ellen Balstad
Illustrators . . . . Laurel Strand, Robin Strobel
Photographer . . . . Brent Kane
Designer . . . . Magrit Baurecht

That Patchwork Place is an imprint of
Martingale & Company.

QUILTS FOR GIRLS AND BOYS: 10 PROJECTS
© 2000 BY BARBARA ROBERTS

MARTINGALE & COMPANY
PO BOX 118
BOTHELL, WA 98041-0118 USA
WWW.PATCHWORK.COM

PRINTED IN THE UNITED STATES OF AMERICA
05 04 03 02 01 00   6 5 4 3 2 1

Mission Statement

We are dedicated to providing quality products and service by working together to inspire creativity and to enrich the lives we touch.

Acknowledgments

I'd like to thank the wonderful people at Martingale & Company for their helpfulness, especially Terry Martin and Dawn Anderson, as well as my editor, Karen Soltys. And what would I do without my wonderful friends who picked up their needles and assisted me with appliquéd tops? They are Penny Clifton, Elisabeth Rollin, Diana Harper, Helen Quane, and Barbara Johnson. Special thanks to Ann Brown Christy, who quilted nearly all the projects in this book with her wonderful style of machine quilting that added so much to each quilt's personality. Thanks also to the folks at my local quilt store, Seminole Sampler, in Catonsville, Maryland, for their support. Another huge thanks to my good friend, Elisabeth Rollin, who has the best color sense this side of heaven and helped me choose all the fabrics in all my quilts— both before and during the writing of this book, and probably after this book, too! A special hug goes to Mimi Dietrich, my friend and fellow quiltmaker. And an "I'm your kiddie" hug goes to my mom, who delights in editing my words, whether they are written or spoken. I'd also like to thank all my students, as well as the people who bought my patterns in the past and have written to me with ideas for even more.

Dedication

This book is dedicated to the special people in my life who have put up with my creative spirit all these years: Jim, Emily, Hanna, and my mom, Pauline Solomon. It is also dedicated to my personal muse, Elizabeth Barrett Browning, whose life and poetry remain an inspiration for me.

Library of Congress Cataloging-in-Publication Data

Roberts, Barbara.
    Quilts for girls and boys / Barbara Roberts.
        p. cm.
    ISBN 1-56477-315-9
        1. Patchwork—Patterns. 2. Quilting—Patterns.
    3. Children's Quilts. I. Title.

TT835.R584 2000
746.46'041—dc21   00-024945

Contents

Preface

When my girls were youngsters years ago, I never had enough time to make special quilts for them. I barely had enough time to sleep! I remember the slow process in the late 1970s of tracing around a triangle template several hundred times with a pencil, cutting each one out individually, and sewing each triangle together by hand. I still have those triangles!

Fortunately, today we have many timesaving tools and methods to complete projects in a reasonable length of time. I know that if I had had a book like this one in the late '70s, with cute and easy designs, I would have completed more quilts. Of course, I also would have had a messier house. When looking back now, I would rather have had the messy house then and some quilts now to remember those precious times with my children—dust bunnies included.

As a quilting teacher, I always try to emphasize to my students the importance of finding their own voice and quilting style. I remind them of children in school who all learn to write the same way. As they grow older, their handwriting changes. They experiment with curves and lines until they develop their own style. As adults, each style is so unique that handwriting experts are needed to identify them. I think this unique style should be the same with quiltmaking. Take pride in your own work and remember that patterns are guidelines, not gospel. I wholeheartedly wish that you will take these patterns and immerse yourselves in them. Explore with color and fabric. If you don't like a curve, change it. If the quilt does not look like the photograph when you finish, do not apologize. Instead, embrace the differences that make you and your quilt unique. Making a quilt should be fun rather than a tedious chore or a situation where we have to make excuses for our finished product. Trust me, there is no such thing as the quilt police. No one will come to your home to confiscate your quilt because it is imperfect!

Don't let anyone steal your joy with criticism, especially yourself.

Finally, with these quilts, try to capture the carefree days of childhood and enjoy the moment. These quilts are fun. The colors can be bright and wonderful and playful. Take your kids with you to the quilt store to choose some fabrics. Let them participate and be involved. They'll get excited over the quilt and the fact that you are making something special just for them.

Introduction

When designing the quilts for this book, I wanted the focus of each quilt to be the child in action rather than the usual ducks, bunnies, and bears that we often see in quilts for children. I hope you find these quilts to be as much fun to make as they were for me to design.

Each of the quilts in this book was made using freezer-paper appliqué, which is my favorite appliqué method. In case you've never tried it yourself, complete instructions for freezer-paper appliqué begin on page 14. I realize, however, that there is more than one way to do most things and appliqué is no exception. Some quiltmakers love needle-turn appliqué, while others love the quick-and-easy technique of fusible appliqué. You'll find instructions for these techniques, too. A combination of

freezer-paper and needle-turn appliqué is found in "The Appliqué Stitch," starting on page 18, and instructions for fusible appliqué begin on page 22. It is important to use an appliqué method that you enjoy so that you are just as happy with the process as you are with the finished quilt.

If you are new to quiltmaking, read through the general directions, which will present different tools and techniques for everything from selecting great fabrics for your project to how to attach a hanging sleeve to a finished wall hanging. If you have appliquéd before, you may want to turn right to the projects section and plunge in. Rest assured that whether you've appliquéd a hundred times before or this is your very first effort, you'll find that all the quilts in this book have nice, easy pieces that will allow you to make your quilt top quickly. Enjoy the journey. Your child, grandchild, niece, or nephew is sure to love the result!

Selecting and Preparing Fabrics

Making quilts for children gives you a wonderful opportunity to play with joyous and wild fabrics that may not make it into your other quilts very often. In fact, to bring out the kid in you and to get your creative juices flowing, you may want to take the child that the quilt is intended for to the quilt shop with you. (If the quilt is for a favorite child who lives far away, call him up and find out what his favorite colors, shapes, and interests are.) Who knows, you may inspire a new generation of quiltmakers!

Like most quilters, I prefer to use 100 percent cotton fabrics for appliqué. They're easy to stitch by hand or fuse, and they're readily available.

Starting with the Main Fabric

Select one multicolored fabric that will be the main fabric to build your color theme around. It might be bright primary colors, such as those in "Blast Off" on page 36. Or wild and crazy limes, turquoises, and hot pinks like those in the "Look Ma, No Hands" quilts on pages 42–43. Just make sure that the colors are fun! Use this fabric to cover a large area, such as a shirt or bike helmet. It will become your focal point with which all additional colors will blend or contrast.

Coordinating Other Fabrics

Next, select coordinating fabrics to fill in the other parts of the quilt. If your multicolored fabric has orange, purple, lime green, and red, you can select these colors for the other fabrics in the quilt. After all, if these colors work together in your main fabric, they will also work together in your quilt. Most of the fabrics needed for appliqué are small, and you may already have some of what you need in your stash. If you need to buy new fabric for appliqué, 1/8 yard of each fabric used in the quilt will be sufficient unless otherwise noted in the fabric requirements for the project.

Also keep in mind the coloring of the child you are making the quilt for. Use matching fabrics for their hair color, skin, eye color, and more. If they love blue, use blues. The quilt can be personalized in many ways to make it unique and special—just like the child you're making it for.

Choosing Border Fabrics

It's easier to select a border fabric while planning your quilt, especially if your color choices cover a wide range of colors. I usually try to select something on the wild side with lots of character. Try to remember who your audience will be.

Picking Background Fabrics

I can't stress enough how important choosing the right background fabric is. The background fabric is a design element that affects the overall look of the quilt. This fabric is placed next to nearly every other fabric you select, and it's necessary for all fabrics to work well together.

You have many choices and options for background fabric, but I recommend a light fabric for beginners to appliqué. A light fabric makes it easier to trace the pattern. And although your fabric can be a solid color, a subtle print or wash of color adds another dimension to the overall look. In the quilts "Whoosh" on page 50 and "Rolling Along" on page 47, notice how the backgrounds swirl from side to side and give these quilts a subtle sense of movement. Look for prints that add movement but that aren't so strong that they overwhelm the design. There are also some nice choices available in white-on-white and cream-on-cream fabrics. A word of caution, however, when working with these fabrics: sometimes the white or cream print on top looks and feels thick and it can be difficult to sew through by hand, making it more of a challenge than you want. Look for a smooth white-on-white or cream-on-cream fabric that you can easily push your needle through if you plan to appliqué or quilt by hand.

A dark background brings the appliqué design

forward and makes the background recede into the distance, such as in the "Blast Off!" quilt on page 36. If the background is a dark color, use lighter colors for the design to provide contrast.

A Word about Print Size

When selecting fabrics for small areas, remember that the amount of fabric used will be small, too. If you choose a print that is large and put it in a small space, it will be out of scale. Instead of seeing a whole flower, you may just see one petal. If you want a flower print, look for a fabric with very tiny flowers. Or you might find that you like the color of the fabric between the flowers. In this case, choose a print with flowers spaced far enough apart that you can cut small pieces from the area between the printed flowers.

Reversing Fabric

One creative option is to use the reverse side of the fabric. This allows you to use the same fabric and color family on your top twice—once as a vibrant color and again as a muted color.

GREAT IDEA!

A great source of fabric for your quilt could be a favorite piece of clothing your child used to wear or is ready to give up. What fun it would be to add it to the quilt and preserve a memory!

Preparing Fabric for Appliqué

All fabrics should be washed in cool water to remove any excess dye. If the water becomes colored, dye is being released. Keep changing the water until it remains clear. Toss the fabric into the dryer on a low heat setting until it is nearly dry, and press the slightly damp fabric with a dry iron until it is completely dry.

If the water never becomes totally clear when washing the fabric, do not use the fabric unless you know with certainty that the quilt will never be washed or get wet. The next time the fabric touches water it will continue to bleed onto the fabrics next to it and onto the background fabric as well.

GREAT IDEA!

If you cannot bear to toss out any fabric, write *Bleeder—Beware* on masking tape and press it securely to the suspect fabric and hide it in your closet. Who knows, maybe in five or ten years a cure will be found and you can take this cloth out of hiding and use it!

Tools and Supplies

In the following section, I've included information about all the possible appliqué supplies you might need. First, you'll find basic supplies for any type of appliqué you do. Next, you'll find things specifically needed for freezer-paper appliqué. Finally, there's a section on the items you'll need if you prefer to do fusible appliqué. Decide which type of appliqué you'd like to do, and read through the supply list to make sure you have all necessary supplies for your preferred appliqué method.

Basic Appliqué

Scissors

Two kinds of scissors are needed for appliqué—a pair for fabric and a pair for freezer paper, fusible web, or plastic templates.

Paper Scissors

Use a pair of good, small paper scissors for cutting out the freezer paper or fusible web. Small scissors work best for this kind of fine work because you need great control to cut into tiny corners and on the lines; the smaller the blade, the more accurate the cut. How do you know when scissors are paper scissors and not fabric scissors? Easy: They can't cut your fabric anymore because they're too dull. Give them a second life. Tie a small ribbon or piece of yarn in one finger hole to distinguish them from sewing scissors. Voilà! They are now your paper scissors.

Fabric Scissors

What is true for paper scissors is also true for fabric scissors. Shears work great when cutting large pieces of fabric but they are too large for fine work such as appliqué. Small fabric scissors that cut sharply all the way to the tips of the blades are essential. Some directions call for snipping fabric to within one or two threads of the line, and this would be difficult to accomplish with dull scissors or with 8" shears.

Fabric Marking Pens

If you are new to appliqué work, you may have missed the great water-soluble, blue-pen controversy. These pens mark fabric with a bright blue line. After you finish your quilt, you dip it in cold water and the lines should disappear. Several years ago it was discovered that, at times, the blue lines would not wash out with water like they were supposed to

do. Or the color would wash out but leave a yellow line where the blue line once was. When you've spent a lot of time working on a quilt and the blue marking lines remain, this can be tragic. Yet there are a number of people that continue to use these water-soluble pens and I am one of them.

When using blue water-soluble pens, I follow four guidelines that have helped and never failed me.

1. Mark with a light touch, and just enough to see what you need to see. Don't press down hard with the pen.
2. Never use the pen when it is running out of ink. You'll know this is happening when you start seeing a lighter shade of blue. If you compensate by pressing harder, the ink toward the bottom of the pen will come out black and won't wash out. (This happened to me once; never again!)
3. *Never* iron over the blue line; you may set the ink.
4. Test the pen on a scrap of the fabric first if you feel the need. You have to remember that rinsing the blue lines out completely may not rid the fabric entirely of the chemicals. Residual chemicals over time may alter the color of the fabric. We have not been using these pens long enough to see what will occur 50 or 100 years down the road. If you are making your once-in-a-lifetime heirloom quilt, it is important to make a decision about these pens before you start.

If you prefer to avoid the water-soluble pen entirely, you can use a fine-lead mechanical pencil, silver marking pencil, chalk, erasable pencil, or any of the other fine marking tools available to quilters.

Another pen I use to draw on the quilt for line definition and tiny details is a Pigma Micron pen made by Sakura Color Products Corporation of Japan. They come in various tip sizes, ranging from .005 to .08. I usually use a .01 tip in either brown, black, blue, or red for drawing on quilts. These pens are available at most quilt shops, quilting mail-order catalogs, and stationery and art supply stores.

Light Box

A light box or light table has a top made of glass or translucent plastic that allows light from below to shine through. Place your pattern on the tabletop and the fabric on top of the pattern. Because the light shines from below, the pattern shows through the fabric and makes it easy to trace the lines onto the fabric. If a dark fabric is used, you will need to mark the fabric with a light color, such as a white or silver marking pencil.

If you don't have a light box, you can create one with a table that slides open in the middle for adding leaves. Separate the table, place a lamp or other light source below the table, place glass or plastic over the opening, and use this as your tabletop.

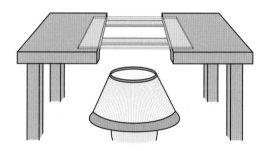

Make your own "light box."

If you don't mind standing to work, another option is to tape your pattern to a window and trace onto the fabric. This is pretty much a daytime option, however, because moonlight doesn't work as well as sunlight.

Sewing Machine

Even for hand appliqué, you'll want your sewing machine nearby so you can sew on borders, attach binding, and maybe even machine quilt your project. For fusible appliqué, you'll need a machine that has a nice zigzag stitch for finishing the raw edges of the appliqués.

Rotary-Cutting Equipment

There must have been a quilting angel listening when we all hungered for an easier method of cutting fabric strips. Rotary cutters, rulers, and self-

GREAT IDEA!

If you don't have a light box or a table that opens, you can place two tables near each other (snack tables, milk crates, or sturdy cardboard boxes work just fine) with a light source on the floor between them. Place your glass or plastic between the two tables to use as a tracing surface.

healing rotary mats make a quilter's life easier and the process of cutting strips more accurate and faster. Even though you cut most of your fabrics with scissors for appliqué, you'll want to have these supplies on hand for cutting background pieces, borders, and binding. Here are the basics on using these tools:

1. Fold the fabric in half, selvages together, matching the lengthwise and crosswise grains.
2. With the folded edge of the fabric closest to you, place it on the cutting mat.
3. To make a 90° right-angle cut, place a square ruler along the folded edge of the fabric. Place a long rotary-cutting ruler against the left side of the square ruler, covering the entire left side of

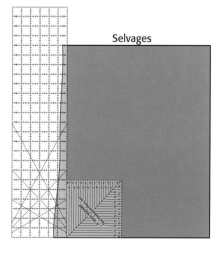

Selvages

the fabric. To save fabric, do this as close to the edge as possible. Make sure the raw edge is completely under the ruler.

4. Remove the square ruler. Place your left hand firmly on the long ruler. Cut the fabric with the rotary cutter by placing the edge of the cutting wheel against the ruler and pressing into the fabric. Roll the cutting edge away from you, along the length of the fabric. Remove and discard the uneven cut strip. If you are left-handed, reverse the above directions.

5. The left fabric edge should now be squared. To

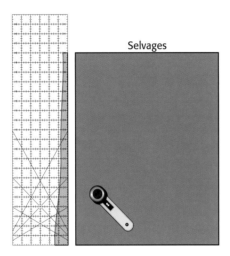

Selvages

make strips for your borders, place your long rotary ruler over the edge of the fabric you just cut. If you need a 3" strip, place the ruler so that the 3" mark lines up along the entire length of the fabric. Cutting away from yourself, cut enough strips to complete the border.

Freezer-Paper Appliqué

Needles

There are many types of needles, all offering a special function. My main concern when choosing a needle is whether I am comfortable with it or not. Some needles are too short to grasp comfortably or are too hard to thread even while wearing my glasses.

Appliqué Needles

I generally work with a Milliner's size 8 needle. The hole is large enough for the thread to go through easily and the length is perfect for my fingers. It is sharp enough to glide through the fabric easily without leaving a gaping hole the size of Montana.

Traditionally, many quilters use Sharps. Sharps in size 11 or 12 are used for sewing when a tiny, close stitch is needed. The higher the number on the needle, the thinner the needle is and the smaller the eye.

Embellishing Needles

In addition to appliqué needles, you'll need larger crewel needles for adding finishing details to the children's faces, fingers, animals, and so on. Crewel needles have eyes large enough to accommodate several strands of embroidery floss.

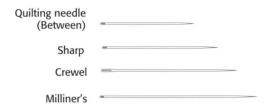

Quilting needle (Between)
Sharp
Crewel
Milliner's

Thread

Select a variety of colors of thread for appliqué, plus white thread for basting if you choose to do freezer-paper appliqué. The following sections describe these two types of threads.

Appliqué Thread

When selecting thread for appliqué, choose colors that match as closely as possible to the color of the fabric you appliqué—*not* the background fabric. If an exact match isn't possible, use a thread color that is one value darker than the fabric, because thread appears lighter when sewing with a single strand than it does on a spool.

Use 100 percent cotton thread in 50 weight whenever possible. It comes in a wide array of colors and is available at most quilting and sewing stores. If cotton isn't available, use cotton-covered polyester.

Remember that sometimes thread is not colorfast and can bleed. Deep colors such as red, blue, and purple have a greater tendency to bleed and cause problems. Be extra careful with these colors. If you need to use a particular thread color and you are concerned, test it for bleeding the same way you would for fabric that bleeds. Cut a few strands and let them soak in a cool water bath. Change the water frequently until no more color comes out. Press them dry with a warm iron to set the color.

Basting Thread

Never use dark thread for basting. The dye from these threads may come off on light-colored fabrics and show up as small dark dots of color that will not come out.

Pins

I love using tiny sequin pins for pinning fabric pieces to the background fabric. They're only about ¾" long, so they don't get in my way when sewing. If you use a large-head pin, it invariably acts as an invisible magnet and your thread gets wrapped around the pinhead, slowing you down. The smaller the head, the smoother the stitching. You also need some long pins (1½" long with yellow heads work well) if you hand-baste your quilt.

Freezer Paper

I love this stuff. It lets you cut very accurate patterns and adheres to your fabric, stabilizing the fabric pieces until you have them stitched securely in place. About ten years ago there was a rumor that freezer paper would disappear from grocery shelves forever. I bought several boxes. It ended up that it was a false rumor, and I still have more than enough left. In addition to finding freezer paper at your supermarket, you can also buy freezer paper made especially for quilters. You'll find it in quilt shops in packages of plain or gridded sheets and boxed rolls.

To use the freezer paper for appliqué, place the uncoated side of the paper face up on top of the pattern piece. Because it is easy to see through, you can trace the design onto the paper with a pencil. Cut out the design with your paper scissors. Be careful to cut accurately on the traced line. Next, place the paper, traced side up, shiny side down, on the wrong side of fabric you selected for the pattern piece. Apply a dry iron to the uncoated side of the paper but do not iron in a back-and-forth motion. Simply press the paper to the fabric. This causes the paper to adhere to the fabric until you wish to remove it, and it will not leave any waxy residue.

Tweezers or Hemostats

Long-nosed tweezers and hemostats are very useful for removing freezer paper from appliquéd pieces. (When you're finished sewing an appliqué piece onto the background, the freezer paper needs to be removed.)

A hemostat has an advantage over tweezers because it has a clamp that locks the tip onto anything placed inside it. Once the freezer paper is locked into the hemostat, all you need to do is pull the paper out, release the clamp, and either throw the paper away or reuse it. Another hemostat advantage is that the tip is rounded and won't poke a hole in your fabric. Hemostats can be bought in medical supply stores or stores that supply tools for doll makers. (For dolls, hemostats are used to turn tiny body parts inside out and to stuff the doll.) They come in several sizes, from very tiny to incredibly huge, and are available with straight or bent tips. Personally, I prefer 6", straight hemostats, but you may find other sizes work better for you.

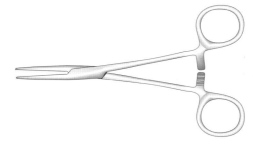

Tracing Paper

The patterns in this book are each printed on more than one page. To make it easy and accurate to trace the entire appliqué design onto your background fabric, it's best to trace the various parts of the pattern onto one sheet of large paper. If your paper isn't large enough, you can tape several pieces together to achieve the size you need. If you use ledger-size tracing paper, you will need about two sheets per quilt design, while smaller tablet-size paper will require several sheets to trace a complete pattern.

As an alternative to tracing the pattern, photocopy the separate pages and then tape them together to create your full-size pattern.

Fusible Appliqué

Fusible Web

If you prefer to fuse your appliqué shapes to the background instead of using freezer paper, you'll need lightweight fusible web. Don't get the heavy-duty type of webbing because you won't be able to sew around the edges with a satin stitch, which is recommended for a nice, finished look.

Thread

Once your shapes have been pressed to the background fabric, it's best to stitch around them to hold them securely and permanently in place. Since you'll be making these projects for children, invariably they'll need to be washed at some point. Don't take chances with the possibility that the fused appliqués might peel; stitch them down.

Thread choices are numerous. You can choose shiny rayons, muted cottons, or even cotton/polyester blends. Choose colors that match the appliqué fabrics exactly. If the exact shade isn't available, choose a shade darker.

Iron

To press your appliqués in place, use a dry iron and follow the manufacturer's directions on the fusible web to determine the heat setting and length of time to press.

Press Cloth

Use a press cloth to prevent any of the glue from the fusible appliqué from getting on your iron or ironing board cover. You can purchase a press cloth or simply use a piece of muslin.

Creating the Appliqué Background

Some of the projects in this book are made with just one fabric background. Others have two main fabrics for backgrounds—usually a sky fabric and something for the ground, such as grass, a street, or a frozen pond. Once you determine the background fabric, sew the sections together, if necessary, and mark the background with the pattern design or use an overlay so that you will know where your appliqué pieces go.

Measuring and Cutting

Use the measurements given in each individual pattern as a guideline. I initially cut my background fabric several inches larger because then I can cut the fabric to the correct size after I have appliquéd. Sometimes I find that the design is not as centered as I would like it to be. With the extra inches available, I can trim more from one side than the other, or more from the top than the bottom, to center the design better. Cutting the background fabric larger than needed is an entirely personal choice. If you prefer to cut the background accurately to start, that's fine, too.

If your background consists of two different fabrics, such as ground and sky, press the seam allowance toward the darker fabric after you sew the pieces together.

Marking the Pattern

In order to know where to start appliquéing on your background, it helps to mark the design directly onto the background fabric. But before you can trace the pattern on the fabric, you will need to find the center of the design. Each design in the book has a mark on the pattern to indicate the center.

Find the center of your background fabric by either folding the fabric into fourths and finger pressing, or by using your ruler to measure the midway point between the length and width. Mark the center lightly.

The full-size patterns for each quilt in this book cover several pages. Each pattern needs to be traced completely onto one sheet of paper before transferring it to the background fabric, to ensure accuracy.

1. Matching up the guidelines, trace the entire pattern onto tracing paper. Either use 2 large ledger-size sheets of tracing paper or several smaller sheets and tape them together.

2. If your background fabric is light enough to see through, you can mark the pattern onto the fabric without using a light box. However, if you cannot see the pattern through the fabric, you will need to have a light source behind the pattern. Place the traced pattern on top of your light box. Matching the center mark on your pattern to the mark on the background fabric, place the fabric on top of the pattern. The center of the pattern needs to be directly underneath the center of the fabric. Tape or pin the fabric to the paper pattern so that it doesn't shift as you work.

3. If you still have difficulty seeing the traced lines of the pattern through your fabric, go over the lines with a permanent marker rather than making a heavy pencil line. If there's too much graphite on your pattern, it will end up rubbing off onto your background fabric.

4. Using a water-soluble marking pen or a mechanical pencil, lightly trace the pattern onto the fabric. Do not reverse the design when marking it onto the fabric. Trace it onto the fabric in the same direction as the pattern in the book.

5. If the fabric is dark, neither a water-soluble pen nor a lead pencil will show. Instead, use a white or silver pencil to trace the design.

An Alternative to Marking

If you don't feel comfortable marking on your background fabric, you can avoid that part of the process by making a pattern overlay.

1. Place your traced copy of the pattern on top of the background fabric so that the center mark in the middle of the design matches up with the mark drawn in the middle of the background fabric. Hold it in place either by taping it down with masking tape or pinning it in place on the top edge of the fabric.

2. When you are ready to start appliquéing onto the background, lift up the overlay and place the first piece down on the fabric, adjusting it until it matches up in the correct spot when the overlay is placed over it.

3. Pin one or more appliqué pieces at a time onto the fabric. You can now stitch onto the background fabric without worrying about covering marking lines or trying to remove ones that show after the appliqué is complete.

Unmarked background fabric

Pattern overlay with traced design

Slide apppliqué shapes under the overlay to place them on the background.

Working with Freezer-Paper Templates

Freezer-paper templates are a great way to make exact duplicates of the shapes in your pattern. They prevent the fabric from stretching out of shape as you sew, thereby letting you match the pieces together perfectly to create the appliqué design. Making and using the templates is easy, and they're even reusable, which makes them great for sharing with an appliqué buddy. There are other options for templates, including making plastic templates and tracing around them onto your fabric for needle-turn appliqué. You can also make your templates from fusible web. (See "Fusible Appliqué: Preparing the Appliqués" on page 22 for details.) I prefer to make my templates from freezer paper and the following sections describe this process.

Making the Templates

Freezer paper is relatively inexpensive, easy to purchase, and each template can be used several times. The most important thing to remember about making freezer-paper templates is that you need to make them in the reverse (mirror image) of the printed pattern because the templates will be pressed to the *wrong* side of the fabric for appliqué. If you make them exactly as they appear on the pattern, they will be facing in the opposite direction of the pattern when you start to appliqué your shapes. For example, in "Ice Dancer" on page 40, the girl is skating toward the right. If you want your finished quilt to have the girl going in this direction, the pattern must be reversed to make the templates. If you want her to be facing left, you must first trace the large master pattern in reverse before marking it on the background fabric and then trace the pattern in the book to make your templates. In "Look Ma, No Hands" on pages 42–46 you'll see two versions of the quilt—one with the child facing right and one with the child facing left. For one quilt I reversed the templates; for the other one I reversed the pattern.

Tracing the Pattern

1. To make all your templates in reverse, take your tracing of the entire pattern (as described on page 13) and flip it over so that it is face down.
2. If the lines aren't dark enough to see clearly through the tracing paper, re-mark the lines on the back side of the tracing paper with a pencil or permanent marker.
3. Place a sheet of freezer paper, shiny side down, on the pattern. Trace around the pattern piece marked #1, taking care to draw exactly on the marked line. Be sure to copy the pattern name and the number of the shape onto the freezer-paper template. (Freezer paper is generally thin enough to see through, but if you have trouble seeing the lines, you can do this step over a light box.)

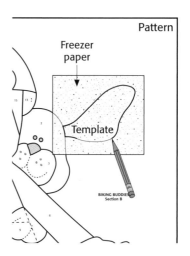

4. Continue tracing all the pattern lines. Follow them as accurately as possible. You don't need to leave space between the templates because you cut them apart exactly on the line. Seam allowances aren't added to the templates.
5. Accurate cutting of the templates is very important. If you cut a curve with a choppy line, you will sew a choppy line. What's more, the pattern piece that butts up to the one where you cut a choppy line will also have that same choppy line!

Adding Markings

As you trace each pattern piece, mark the following information on each template:

1. *Project name.* This will come in handy if you make more than one project from the book or if you plan to reuse the patterns in the future. At a glance, you can tell which quilt the templates are for.

2. *Pattern number.* Underline 6s and 9s to avoid confusion later.

3. *Pattern name.* Write down what each piece is, such as the dog's ear or the right sleeve.

Cutting the Fabric Appliqués

Although the templates are not small enough to toss as confetti, you will probably feel like celebrating at this point. All the black-and-white grunt work is done and it's time to have fun with color.

After the templates are cut out, they are ready to be pressed onto your selected fabrics. Using a hot, dry iron, press each template onto the wrong side of the appropriate fabrics, leaving at least 1" between the templates if you are cutting more than one shape from a fabric.

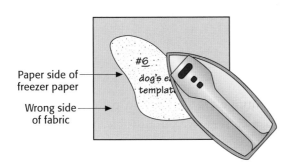

Paper side of freezer paper →

Wrong side of fabric →

If possible, press the longest part of the template onto the bias of the fabric. The bias has the most stretch and give, which will make it easier to turn the edges under for basting. It also helps the appliqué to lie flatter than if it were cut on the straight of grain.

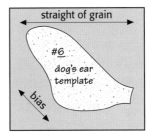

Using your fabric scissors, cut out the fabric approximately ¼" from the edge of the freezer paper along all edges that will be finished (basted back) and ½" from the freezer paper on edges that will remain flat (unbasted). Flat edges are overlapped by other fabric pieces, which will hide the unbasted edge.

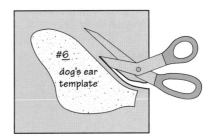

With your marked background fabric placed on a flat surface, you can plan the color placement of the quilt by placing each numbered template with fabric attached over the marked corresponding number. Sometimes a color combination that looked great on the cutting table in the quilt shop doesn't work when it is placed next to other fabrics in your design at home. Now is the time to experiment and be pleased with your work. It is easier to select another fabric now than it is after you sew the pieces together. (Although you can do that, too!)

To change fabrics, simply peel the template off the fabric and press it onto another fabric with your iron. When you are pleased with all your fabric choices, it's time to start basting.

Basting the Templates

When I was new to appliqué, I would turn under and baste all the finished edges. I preferred to baste everything in sight. Today, with more experience, I prefer a combination of basting and needle turning. Instructions on needle-turn appliqué with freezer-paper templates as a guide are provided in "Needle-Turning" on pages 19–20. Most of the pattern pieces for this book are large and have easy, gentle curves. For these pieces, I needle turn them. For the smaller pieces that have sharper curves and inside points, I baste them. The more you sew and become comfortable with your skill level, the more you will enjoy the challenge of skipping most of the basting and going right into appliqué.

Practice Basting

The best shape to use to practice basting and appliquéing is a heart. A heart has straight lines, curves, and both an inside and outside point. In short, it has everything you need!

Heart pattern for basting practice

1. Trace the heart above onto freezer paper. Cut out the heart and press it to the wrong side of a scrap fabric.
2. Cut out the fabric heart. Make sure to cut ¼" away from the edge of the freezer paper so that you'll have a ¼" seam allowance.

3. Cut an 18" piece of thread. Thread your needle, double the thread, and knot the ends. Use white thread on medium and light fabrics, and gray on dark fabrics. You will want to start stitching from the top of your appliqué. This way the knot will be on top, which will make it easier to remove the basting thread when you finish appliquéing.
4. With the right side of the fabric facing you, hold the heart so that you'll be stitching toward the bottom point. With your thumb and index finger, fold the ¼" seam allowance along the straight edge of the heart over the freezer-paper template on the back. Insert the needle from the top and pull the thread through to the back.
5. While basting on a straight edge, your stitches

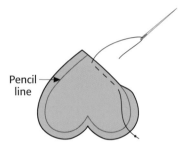

Pencil line

can be longer—about ¼" apart. About ½" before you get to the bottom tip of the heart, fold back the tip onto the freezer paper so that your heart looks like it has a flat bottom. Next, fold the side where you are stitching over the first fold and continue basting to the point and stop.

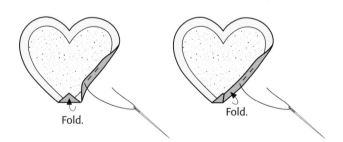

Fold.   Fold.

6. Fold the second straight edge over the folded tip and continue to baste on the other straight-edge side to the top of the heart.

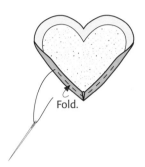

Fold.

7. Continue basting with ¼" stitches until you reach the first curve. As you go around the curve, begin to take smaller basting stitches, smoothing the seam allowance over the edge of the freezer paper. If you find that you are getting bumps in the fabric rather than a smooth curve, you may be turning too much fabric over (exceeding the ¼" seam allowance recommendation), or trying to go around the curve with stitches that are too far apart. You can remedy the situation by trimming the fabric seam allowance a bit and by taking shorter stitches. If any bumps still remain in this area, you can smooth them out when you do the actual appliquéing by pushing the excess fabric behind the template with the tip of your needle.

8. As you approach the inside point at the top of the heart, carefully clip the fabric with the tip of your fabric scissors to within two threads of the freezer paper.

Clip.

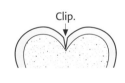

9. Hold the fabric down on either side of the inside point and baste the ¼" margin down. Continue around the other top curve of the heart and back to where you started.

Keep stitches small around curves.

GREAT IDEA!

If you baste close to the edge of the freezer paper ($\frac{1}{16}$" to $\frac{1}{8}$" from the edge), it is easier to make the seam allowances that are turned under lie flat and smooth. If you baste farther away, you'll have more bulk to manage.

Basting with Curves

There are two kinds of curves. Convex curves are like the curve around the outside of a cookie. They are never clipped. Concave curves are like the inside curve you find when you take a bite out of that cookie! Concave curves are always clipped so that the seam allowance fans out behind the template and lies flat.

While it's necessary to clip concave curves for smooth-looking appliqué, remember to always clip them with just the tips of your scissors so that you don't slip and cut into your appliqué. And, don't make the clips until you reach the curved section. Otherwise, they can fray from being handled.

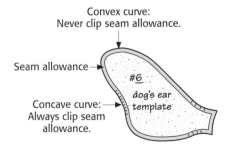

Convex curve:
Never clip seam allowance.

Seam allowance

#6
dog's ear template

Concave curve:
Always clip seam allowance.

The Appliqué Stitch

There are many wonderful methods of appliqué. I cover my favorite method here (which I was fortunate to learn from my friend and appliqué teacher, Mimi Dietrich). If you'd like to try other appliqué techniques—either by hand or machine—I highly recommend *The Easy Art of Appliqué* (That Patchwork Place, 1994), an excellent book by Mimi Dietrich and Roxi Eppler. It explains in depth numerous methods of hand and machine appliqué. You can experiment and choose your favorite technique.

Appliquéing the Pieces

The appliqué stitch is the same whether or not you baste edges on your pieces. The pattern pieces are stitched in numerical order, with each consecutive piece overlapping the ones before it.

1. Pin the basted piece #1 onto the background fabric, matching it to the lines you traced from the large master pattern.
2. Using thread that matches the appliqué fabric, thread the needle and knot one end.
3. To hide the knot, place the needle in the fold of your pattern piece between the freezer paper and the folded-over seam allowance. Have your needle come out at the fold, but don't pull so hard that the knot pops through the fabric.
4. Place the needle into the background fabric on the traced pattern line as close as possible to the pattern piece. Stitching parallel to the traced line, glide the tip of the needle ⅛" to ¼", coming out of the background fabric and going back into the fold of the seam allowance of your appliqué piece. You want to catch about 2 threads of the fold and come out again. If your needle goes only into the fold of the appliqué, your stitches will become nearly invisible. If your needle takes up more than 2 threads of fabric, you'll stitch deeper into the appliqué, and your stitches will be more likely to show on top of the appliqué.

GREAT IDEA!

Cut your piece of appliqué thread so that it's 12" to 18" long. The longer your thread, the more it tends to tangle and knot. Plus, the section of the thread that lies within the eye of the needle starts to wear, grow thin, and split. If you start with shorter thread, you won't place so much stress on the same part of thread for too long. When appliquéing your pieces, never use a portion of the thread where it has split. You don't want to include a weak point in your work.

5. Go back into the background fabric on the traced pattern line as close as possible to the pattern piece. Again, glide the needle only a short distance underneath the fabric and come out into the fold of the appliqué. Having your needle move along under the background fabric aids in hiding your stitches.

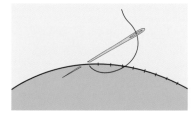

Appliqué stitch

6. Rather than knot off the appliqué thread when a piece is completed, bring the needle to the back side of the work and make 3 small backstitches close to your stitching. Next, bury the tail of the thread by sticking the needle into the back of the quilt top only (be careful that it doesn't come out

on top of your appliqué), parallel to the line of stitching just completed. Glide the needle about 1" and bring the needle out on the back again. Clip the thread close to the fabric.

7. After each piece is completely stitched in place, remove the basting stitches. Once the thread has been pulled out, you can remove the freezer-paper template with your tweezers or hemostat. For more information on this, see "Removing the Templates" on page 21.

Stitching Inside and Outside Points

Just as there are two types of curves (concave and convex), there are two types of points that you encounter in appliqué—inside and outside. Let's use our heart example to illustrate how to achieve perfect points in both cases. For illustration purposes, the edges of the heart have been left unbasted.

Inside Points

1. Stitch to within ¼" of the inside point at the top of the heart and stop.
2. Take the other side of the heart, which has not yet been stitched, and fold it down as shown in the illustration.
3. Sew *exactly* to the point, and take 2 tiny stitches.
4. Unfold the unstitched side of the heart and continue appliquéing.

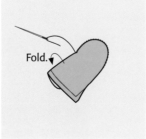

Outside Points

1. Start sewing the appliqué along a straight edge.
2. Sew all the way to the tip of the point.
3. Take 2 very tiny stitches next to each other at the point.
4. With the tip of your needle, push the seam allowance from the other side of the point firmly underneath the template where you have just stitched.
5. Continue stitching along the other side of the point, as before.

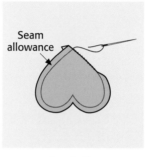
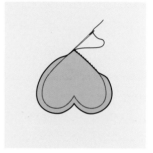

Sew to tip.

Push seam allowance under with the tip of your needle.

Needle Turning

If you decide to leave any of the edges unbasted on your appliqués, stitch them in the same way as described in "Stitching Inside and Outside Points." Use your needle to turn under the edges as you go because they haven't been basted under. The following steps describe needle turning.

1. Using the side of the tip of your needle, push the fabric seam allowance underneath the freezer-paper template. The stiffness of the template helps to keep the shape of each pattern piece as you nudge the seam allowance against it with your needle.
2. When the seam allowance has been pushed under the template, hold it in place between the thumb and index finger of your nonsewing

hand. Your thumb will be on the top of the background fabric and the rest of your hand will be underneath the fabric.

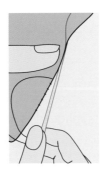

Push seam allowance under
with tip of needle.

3. On straight edges, you can fold under about ½" of the seam allowance at a time and stitch it in place. As you go around curves, however, use your needle more often to turn under the seam. Take very close stitches as you round a curve. The closer the stitches, the smoother the curve. Use your needle to push under any loose or frayed threads that result from snipping into the seam allowance. Use your needle and thread to enclose these areas with stitches that are very close to each other.

GREAT IDEA!

Don't worry about turning under a long portion of the seam allowance at one time. You'll find it's easiest to ease the seam allowance in place if you turn under only about ¼" to ½" at a time.

Basting Appliqué Pieces

Sometimes a large appliqué pattern piece calls for a flat edge (not basted or turned under) that is several inches long because an overlapping fabric will hide the edge. By leaving the edge flat, you reduce bulk in your appliqué because you don't have two layers of fabric under another appliqué—just one flat edge. Edges that won't be covered by an overlapping fabric need to be finished. Some pieces will have both basted edges and flat edges. You'll also have some pieces where all edges are finished and some where all edges are flat. For an example, refer to pages 55–57 for "Biking Buddies" piece #1, where the dog's ear is overlapped by piece #2, the dog's head. The fabric around the ear, except on the bottom edge, needs to be turned under with a basting stitch to give a finished edge. The remaining bottom edge of the ear should be left as a flat edge because it will be overlapped by piece #2 and won't show.

As with all the flat edges, you will eventually have another fabric appliquéd over it, but until then it is simply a loose edge. As you stitch other appliqués in place, this fabric tends to bunch up and can result in a puckered area.

To prevent puckering, baste the raw edge of the appliqué in place on the background fabric with the same thread you used to appliqué the piece. The basting stitches can be pulled out later or left in. They won't be visible because they will be covered by the overlapping appliqué piece.

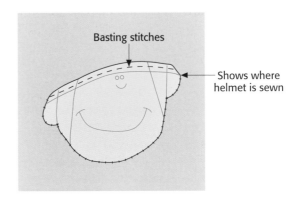

Removing the Templates

After each individual pattern piece is stitched in place, the freezer paper needs to be removed. You can use your fingers, tweezers, or hemostat for this step. Removing the freezer paper is easy when you have an open, flat edge through which to pull it. (If you're going to baste the flat edges in place, be sure to remove the freezer paper first!) Gently separate the freezer paper from the fabric before tugging on it so that you don't tear or gather the appliqué stitches. Occasionally, you will have pattern pieces that have finished edges all around. With these, you have two options for removing the freezer paper.

Option 1

As you near the last ½" of stitches, pull out the basting thread and remove the freezer paper. Do this on a straight edge if possible. It is easier to sew a straight line than a curved line once the template is removed. Never attempt this feat at a point!

Option 2

Stitch the entire pattern piece in place. Remove the basting thread, flip the quilt top over to the back, and make a small slit *very carefully* in the center of the just-stitched area. Make the slit large enough to insert your tweezers or hemostat tips so that you can grab the freezer paper and remove it. Cutting into your background fabric does not weaken it. If you think about it, patchwork quilts are a series of separate fabrics sewn together with a ¼" margin and they don't fall apart. Why should this? Don't bother whipstitching the opening. This will just make a lump under your appliqué.

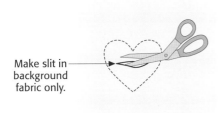

Make slit in background fabric only.

Cutting Away the Background Fabric

During the appliqué process, you may have as many as three or four different fabrics overlapping in the same area. This creates a bulky area that is always difficult to quilt through by hand. The easiest way to deal with this situation is to cut away the background fabric. Don't worry. Cutting away the background from an appliquéd area before you add the next appliqué does not harm your quilt. If you leave a ¼" margin around the cutout area, it will not rip apart. Now when you appliqué the next piece to the quilt top, rather than sewing through several layers of fabric, you sew through just one. The only time you'll have to sew through multiple layers is right where the seam allowances of two pieces overlap.

Another advantage to cutting away the background fabric can be seen when a lighter fabric is sewn over a darker one. Sometimes the darker fabric is visible through the lighter top fabric and changes the color of the lighter fabric to a few shades darker. I find this is especially true when I appliqué a light-color skin-tone fabric over a bright color, such as green grass. If you cut away the background fabric, this problem is eliminated.

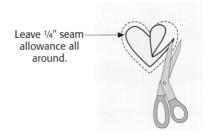

Leave ¼" seam allowance all around.

Cut away background fabric only.

Re-marking Pattern Lines

If your pattern has pieces that are to be sewn over another appliqué, marked guidelines on the background for lining up the pieces on top will not be visible once you stitch the bottom appliqué in place. For an example, turn to "Biking Buddies" on page 32. In this quilt, once you stitch the dog's head onto the background, you won't be able to see the markings for his face. You can re-mark those guidelines in one of two ways:

• Place the master paper pattern on your light table with the quilt top over it. Match the pattern to the drawn lines on the background fabric. If you can see the pattern lines through the dog's head, use a marking pen or pencil and re-mark the lines onto the dog's head.
• If you cannot see the lines through the fabric layers, take the basted face and place it over the dog's head. Refer to the pattern for guidance and re-mark the lines. You can also simply pin the face in place and refer to the pattern and quilt photograph for reference.

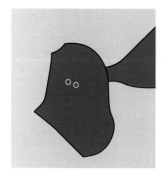
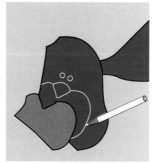

Fusible Appliqué

While hand appliqué with freezer paper can be a relaxing and rewarding process, sometimes you may want to make a quilt in a hurry. When that's the case, fusible web is a great option. Instead of hand stitching each appliqué in place, this material glues your appliqués in place. Because these projects are for kids, I recommend machine stitching around each appliqué piece to make sure it's secure and can stand up to washing.

Preparing the Appliqués

Making fusible-web templates is similar to making them from freezer paper.

1. First, trace each pattern piece in reverse onto the paper-backing side of the fusible web. Unlike freezer paper, however, do not trace them directly side by side. Leave about ½" between templates as you trace.
2. With your paper scissors, cut out around each shape. Cut roughly ¼" outside the drawn line.
3. Press the fusible-web shapes onto the *wrong* side of the appropriate appliqué fabrics with a dry iron. Refer to the manufacturer's directions for how long to press and the proper heat setting. Don't press longer than is recommended or the bond won't hold.
4. Cut out the appliqués exactly on the drawn line.

Attaching Appliqués to Background

Prepare your background fabric and trace the master appliqué pattern onto the background fabric, as described on pages 12–13. However, do not use the blue water-soluble pen to make the marks because an iron is used to press your appliqués onto the background. The heat of the iron will heat-set the markings and make them impossible to wash out. Use a lead pencil and trace very lightly. To make sure your pieces cover the markings, trace slightly inside the pattern lines so you don't have to worry about washing out markings later.

1. Lay out all your appliqué pieces to make sure you're happy with the fabrics you've selected. Now is the time to make any changes if you're not satisfied.
2. Peel the paper backing off the appliqués. If you have a hard time peeling the paper away from the edge, score the paper in the center with the tip of a pin, and you can easily lift the paper away from the appliqué.
3. Place the appliqués back on the background, starting with piece #1. Press the appliqués to the background in numerical order. Let the fabric cool before pressing each new piece.
4. Continue adhering pieces to the background until all are attached.

GREAT IDEA!

Your quilt top can get quite stiff from all the fusible web. So, for large pieces, it's best to cut away the center of the fusible-web template before you iron it to the fabric. To do this, trace the templates as described in the preceding section. Cut them out roughly ¼" outside the drawn line. Also cut away the excess fusible web by cutting ¼" *inside* the marked line as shown. After you iron the fusible web to the fabric, cut only the appliqué shape on the drawn line. Only the outer edges of each shape will have fusible web, and your finished quilt will be lighter and less stiff.

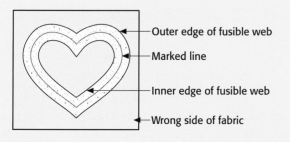

Outer edge of fusible web
Marked line
Inner edge of fusible web
Wrong side of fabric

Satin Stitching around Appliqués

A narrow, machine zigzag stitch gives your quilt a more finished look and keeps the pieces permanently in place, even if the quilt is washed. Satin-stitch around the shapes in the order that you appliqué them. Shapes that are overlapped by others don't need to be stitched completely around; you only need to stitch the part that shows.

1. Set your machine stitch width to a narrow zigzag. You want to finish the raw edges of the appliqués but not overwhelm the design.
2. Change the thread so that your stitches always match the fabric you're appliquéing.
3. Start stitching with the needle to the right swing of the zigzag stitch. Turn the fly wheel so that the needle enters the background fabric, right next to the appliqué. Then, when you start stitching, the swing to the left will be in the appliqué. You want the stitches to go primarily into the appliqué and not too far into the background fabric.

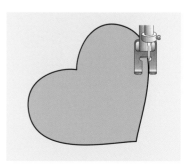

Needle to right of appliqué
in background fabric

4. When you come to an outer point, stitch to the point and stop with the needle just off the point in the *right* swing position. Lift the presser foot and pivot your work. Turn the fly wheel manually to get the needle in the *left* swing position, with the needle in the appliqué, not in the background. Lower the presser foot and begin stitching.

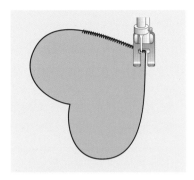

Pivot fabric, put needle in left position in fabric, and resume stitching.

5. For inside corners, stitch until your needle is as far away from the inside corner as the width of your zigzag stitch. Stop with the needle in the *left* position so that it is in the appliqué fabric. Pivot your fabric so you are ready to sew the next side of the corner. Manually turn the fly wheel until the needle swings to the right position. Position the needle back in the appliqué fabric and you're ready to start stitching.

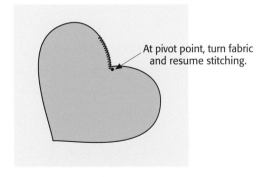

At pivot point, turn fabric and resume stitching.

6. For curves, your stitching looks best if you stop and pivot the fabric slightly every few stitches as you go. For convex curves, pivot when the needle is to the left and inside the appliqué fabric. For concave curves, pivot when the needle is to the right and in the background fabric.

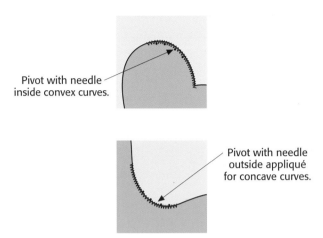

Pivot with needle inside convex curves.

Pivot with needle outside appliqué for concave curves.

7. When you've gone completely around a shape, cut the threads, thread them through a hand-sewing needle, and pull them to the back of your work. Tie the top and bobbin threads together to knot them and clip off the tails.

Finishing Techniques

Here you are. All the appliquéing is done. Your top looks wonderful. You feel smug, naturally. But before you can consider your quilt done, you actually have to finish it. If you've never made a quilt before, or if you'd like a little guidance to perfect your finishing techniques, read through this section for help in everything from adding borders that fit perfectly to marking the quilting designs or adding final embroidery details.

Borders

Borders can enhance, enclose, and finish the look of an appliqué top. Of course, some people may choose to ignore borders, which isn't a problem. But if you want borders, here's how to measure, cut, and stitch them for a perfect fit.

Fabric Selection

Border fabrics usually coordinate with the colors in the quilt. Choose fabrics that can help make the quilt more appropriate for a child, which should be easy because there are some really great, kid-friendly choices available today. If the fabric you choose has a directional print, such as stripes, you need to plan ahead regarding the direction of the print. And, if you use directional border fabric, factor in additional fabric beyond the measurements recommended in the project directions for matching patterns such as stripes or plaids.

Measuring and Sewing on Borders

If you make any changes in size to the background fabric, you cannot use the border measurements provided in each project. I like to cut my background slightly oversized and then trim it to the size called for in the project directions so that it is perfectly square and ready for borders.

GREAT IDEA!

Use less border fabric by cutting the borders for the shorter edges of the quilt first (as long as this measurement is less than 21"). For example, if you have fabric that is 42" wide and one of the measurements of the quilt is 21" or less, you can cut two border strips from just one strip, thereby eliminating the need to cut four strips for borders. Now you can cut just three!

Here is how to determine what size of border strips to cut:

1. Measure through the center of the quilt top, from one side to the other. Cut 2 border strips to this measurement. (Remember to remove the selvages from the border-fabric strips.) Sew these borders to the top and bottom of the quilt, easing fabric as necessary. Using a dry iron, press the borders flat and press the ¼" seam allowances toward the border fabric.

2. Measure through the center of the quilt, from the outer edge of the top border to the bottom border's outer edge. Cut 2 border strips to this measurement and sew them to the sides of the quilt, again easing fabric as necessary. Measuring through the center of the quilt and cutting the borders the same length keeps the quilt's outer measurements consistent and square, and prevents wavy borders. Press the seam allowances toward the border fabric.

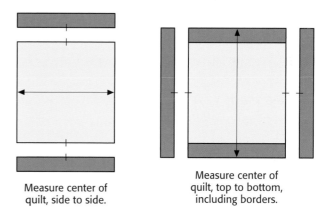

Measure center of quilt, side to side.

Measure center of quilt, top to bottom, including borders.

Embroidery Techniques

Each of my quilts contains a small amount of embroidery to enhance facial features for the children, dogs, cats, and more. See the individual quilt instructions for when to use each type of stitch. I use four basic stitches in my quilts.

Stem stitch: Use this stitch wherever lines are needed on the quilt top.

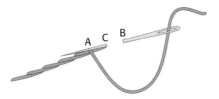

Chain stitch: This stitch is wider and more decorative than a stem stitch.

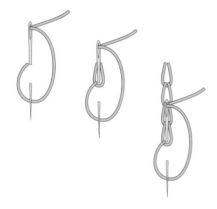

Satin stitch: This stitch is used to fill in large areas, such as eyes and noses. It covers an area completely.

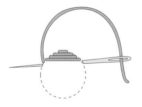

French knot: I always use this stitch for freckles.

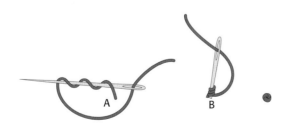

Adding Other Details

An alternative to embroidering details is to use Sakura Pigma Micron pens in brown, black, blue, and red. Although this gives details a flat appearance compared to embroidery, it is a great way to save time yet still add details.

I guess it is the doll maker in me, but I can't resist giving my little people on my quilts rosy cheeks and sometimes a rosy nose. I have some powdered blush that I apply very gently to the quilt with a cotton puff or my fingertip. This is the very last step because powder tends to disappear if you handle the quilt too much.

Another alternative you can use for adding details is colored pencils. Berol Prismascolor colored pencils work the best because the lead is soft and blends into fabric well. Test these products on scraps of fabric before applying them to your quilt to make sure you like the results.

Quilt Backing

When it comes to backing fabric for the quilt, you have lots of choices. You can go to your local quilt store and find the ugliest fabric in the bargain bin and use it as a backing because "it's so cheap." Or you can select a fabric that either reflects the color scheme of the front, or maybe the theme of the quilt. The decision is yours, but ask yourself whether you want to cringe each time the quilt flips over or would rather have a back that is as lovely as the front.

No Show-Through

One thing to keep in mind when selecting a quilt backing is how dark the fabric is and whether or not it could show through to the front of your quilt. If your quilt top has a light background, it may be risky to use a very dark backing fabric. To be sure, take your quilt top and a piece of batting to the quilt shop. Layer them on the cutting table and make sure that the quilt backing doesn't show through to the front.

Cutting the Backing

I like to cut my backing fabric several inches larger than my appliquéd top. Sometimes the fabric will shift, or it may pucker from the quilting. If you cut the backing the same size as the quilt top and puckers occur, the backing fabric will be too short and you'll need to trim the whole quilt before adding binding. If you add extra inches to the backing, you can trim the backing fabric when you're finished quilting without having to trim the top, too.

Batting

Batting is the layer of the quilt that goes between the appliquéd top and the backing fabric. Think of it as the filling in your quilt "sandwich." For small wall quilts like the projects in this book, I prefer to use very thin batting, such as Thermore, which is a polyester batting. You can use a thin cotton batting, too. Thin batting makes the quilting process easier and I can make tinier stitches. Cut the batting the same size as the backing fabric, allowing for several extra inches to be trimmed after quilting.

Marking the Top

Before you baste the three layers of the quilt together, you need to make another important design choice. Do you want to mark quilting lines on your top? If so, do you plan to trace these lines from a printed pattern (your own or a published pattern) or use a stencil to mark them?

If you choose your quilting design from a book or from another source, it is easier to mark the top of your quilt before basting. Place the pattern and quilt top on your light box and trace lightly with a marking tool such as a water-soluble ink marker, chalk, erasable quilting pencil, or silver marking pencil. Always use a light touch.

If you plan on stenciling the pattern onto your quilt top, you can mark your quilt before or after basting. Quilt shops and mail-order sources can provide you with lots of interesting stencils. The stencil

is placed on the quilt top. With your marking tool, draw inside the lines on the stencil. These become your quilting lines. After you have finished quilting and if you used a water-soluble ink pen, soak your quilt in cool water until all the ink is removed. (I hope you didn't use fabric that bleeds!)

Basting the Quilt Layers

Quilts are composed of three layers: the finished top, the batting, and the backing fabric. Before you begin quilting, you need to baste the three quilt layers together to keep them from shifting during the quilting process. You can baste your quilt with needle and thread, with safety pins, or even with a quilt tacking system. If you use the latter, refer to the manufacturer's directions.

Hand Basting

Tape the backing fabric, wrong side up, to a flat work surface with masking tape. Center the batting over the fabric and smooth it out with your hands. Finally, place the appliquéd top, right side up, over the other two layers.

With long straight pins, pin the three layers together to hold them secure while you baste. Any needle that is long with a sharp point will do. You want to use long pieces of thread (light colors only) and sew long running stitches. Baste an **X** through the center of the quilt first. Next, baste parallel lines vertically and horizontally through the quilt. Your parallel lines can be 3" to 6" apart, depending upon how secure you prefer your layers to be. All basting stitches will be removed when quilting is completed.

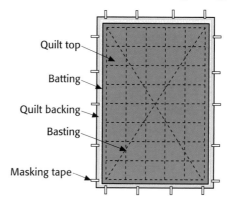

Quilt top
Batting
Quilt backing
Basting
Masking tape

Pin Basting

Safety pins can be a substitute for hand basting. Layer your quilt as described in "Hand Basting" above. Next, start pinning in the center of the quilt. Use rust-free safety pins made for quilting. The #2 size is used most often, but for a finer safety pin, use size #1. Work your way to the outside edges, smoothing the three layers as you go along to avoid any bunching in either the front or the back of the quilt. This method is a lot quicker than basting with thread, but the pins often get in your way and grab onto your quilting thread if you're hand quilting. To avoid this, you can pin from the back. Safety pins are easy to remove if they get in the way while machine quilting. They're easier to remove than basting thread, too, which invariably ends up getting stitched over if you machine quilt.

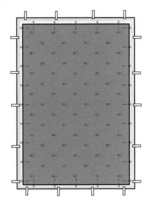

Quilting

The actual stitching that is done to hold the three layers together is called quilting. How much quilting you do is an individual choice. In addition to this sewing being functional, it can also be beautiful. It can give direction and movement to your backgrounds, emphasize the appliquéd design, and add pictures to your borders. You can quilt your project by hand or machine.

Hand-Quilting Basics

If you quilt by hand, the stitch is just an easy running stitch. You want to keep your stitches of even length and even spacing.

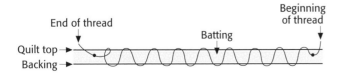

To begin, put your quilt in a quilting hoop or use a quilting frame. This provides even but not-too-tight tension on the layers and holds your quilt taut for hand quilting. Next, make sure that the thread you have is made and marked for quilting. Hand-quilting thread is stronger than regular sewing thread; it may or may not be coated. Cut a piece of thread about 18" long, thread the needle (most quilters prefer to use Betweens), and knot one end. From the top of your quilt, pull your needle and thread through until the knot pops inside the quilt layers. Leave the knot buried inside to hide it.

I like to start quilting in the center of the quilt, stitching around the appliquéd shapes. As you move into the areas that are just background fabric, you can stitch marked designs or use free-form quilting—quilting wherever you want in random patterns. On "Biking Buddies" on pages 32–33, I used a drinking glass and kept marking around the bottom of the glass onto the quilt top and overlapping circles in a pattern I liked.

Machine Quilting

If you prefer machine quilting, that's fine, too. Many of the quilts in this book have been machine quilted. Take a close look at them for ideas on how to quilt your projects.

To machine-quilt, use a walking foot. Set your stitch length a little longer than what you use for patchwork so that the stitches have room to go through all layers. Or, you can use a darning foot, lower the feed dogs on your machine, set the stitch length to 0, and use free-motion stitching. With free-motion quilting, you move the quilt to make the stitches instead of having the machine feed the fabric for you.

Don't use hand-quilting thread for machine quilting. Look for machine-quilting threads, which are heavier than sewing thread but made to flow through your machine's tension system.

Trimming the Quilted Layers

When you finish quilting the three layers together, lay them on your cutting table on top of your rotary-cutting mat. With your rotary cutter and ruler, trim the excess batting and backing fabric so that all three layers are the same size and the quilt edges are straight.

Binding

There are several ways to bind a quilt, but my favorite is double-fold or French binding cut on the straight grain of the fabric. To learn more about other binding methods, I recommend *Happy Endings* (That Patchwork Place, 1987) by Mimi Dietrich for an excellent reference describing other binding and edge-finishing treatments.

1. For a French binding that is ⅜" wide when finished, measure around the outside of your quilt and add 9" to that measurement to determine the length of binding you need. For instance, if your quilt is 21" x 28", the perimeter would measure 98". Add 9" to that for a total of 107". Divide this sum by the width of your binding fabric (42") and round up to the nearest whole number to get the number of strips to cut. In our example, 107" divided by 42" equals 2½. Round up to 3 strips.

2. Cut binding strips 2½"-wide across the width of the fabric from selvage to selvage. Cut off the selvages. They add bulk and don't give like the rest of the fabric does.

3. Join the strips end to end to make the total length needed. Fold one end of the binding strip over to form a 45° angle as shown. Then fold the binding strip in half lengthwise, wrong sides together, and press.

Fold line

4. Starting at the folded end of the binding, match the raw edges of the binding to the cut edges of the quilt. Beginning about 6" from one corner,

sew the binding to the quilt with a ⅜"-wide seam allowance. Sew to within ⅜" from the edge; backstitch.

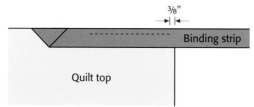

⅜"

Binding strip

Quilt top

5. For a mitered corner, fold the binding away from the quilt as shown, creating a 45° angle. Fold the binding back over the quilt, matching raw edges. Stitch, beginning at the edge of the quilt as shown. Stitch to within ⅜" from the next corner. Stop stitching and then backstitch. Repeat to miter all corners in the same fashion.

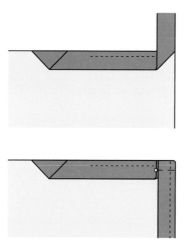

6. When you reach the point where you began stitching, trim away the extra binding. Tuck the end of the binding inside the folded end as shown. Stitch past your starting stitches and backstitch.

7. Turn the binding over the raw edges on the back of the quilt. Make sure the folded edge of the binding covers the stitching on the back of the quilt. Hand stitch the folded edge of the binding to the quilt.

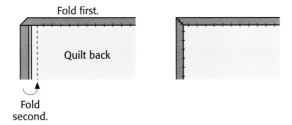

Fold first.

Quilt back

Fold second.

If you want a binding width other than ⅜", adjust the width of the strips you cut. The quilts in this book assume that you start with 2½"-wide binding strips and require ¼ yard of fabric. You may need to adjust the yardage requirements if you change the binding width.

Attaching a Hanging Sleeve

Sewing a hanging sleeve to the back of your quilt is always a good idea. You never know how a quilt will be used when you give it as a gift. It might end up on the wall or on a bed. Either way, it will be ready for display. I like to make hanging sleeves out of the same material that I use for the quilt backing. Plan ahead so that you'll have enough leftovers for a matching sleeve.

1. Cut a strip of fabric that measures 10" wide and 1" less than the width of the quilt.
2. Fold the strip in half along the length, with right sides together. Stitch the raw edges together using a ¼" seam.
3. Turn the sleeve right side out and press so that the sleeve seam runs along the center of one side of the sleeve and not along either edge.

4. Fold the raw edges of the sleeves under ¼". Fold again and stitch the hem in place.

5. Place the seam side of the sleeve against the back of the quilt and pin the sleeve at the top of the quilt so that it's top edge is just below the edge of the binding. Hand stitch across the top of the sleeve. Make sure that your stitches don't show on the front of the quilt.
6. In order to provide some extra room for the rod to slip into the sleeve without pulling on the quilt, raise the lower edge of the sleeve up about ½" and slipstitch the bottom of the sleeve to the back of the quilt. Again, check to make sure that you do not stitch through to the front of the quilt.

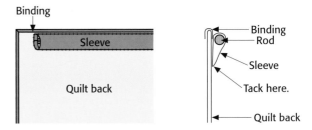

Binding

Sleeve

Quilt back

Binding
Rod

Sleeve

Tack here.

Quilt back

Labeling Your Quilt

You've just sewn a miniature masterpiece. It will be handed down from the original recipient for generations to come. It will probably be someone's comfort blanket and will be taken along when the first colony is developed on Mars. Years later, it will be featured in the Mars Museum of History as an early example of textiles imported to the New World. But alas, you won't get the credit if your name doesn't appear anywhere on the quilt. Nor will the year or place of origin be known. What a tragedy. All because you didn't take the time to make and attach a label.

I have only three things to say to you:
1. Label your quilt.
2. Label your quilt.
3. Label your quilt.

To make your label extra special, include your name, location, and date, but also whom the quilt was made for and the occasion, such as birth, birthday, or the first day of school. The recipient will feel extra special—just as you intended.

THE QUILTS

BIKING BUDDIES (GIRL) was designed by Barbara Roberts, 1999, Catonsville, Maryland, 28" x 35½". Appliquéd by Penny Clifton and machine quilted by Ann Brown Christy.

Biking Buddies

What could be more fun that racing off on your bike on a Saturday afternoon with Fido or Spot along for the ride! Adapt this quilt for your favorite bike-riding boy or girl.

FINISHED QUILT SIZE: 28" x 35½"

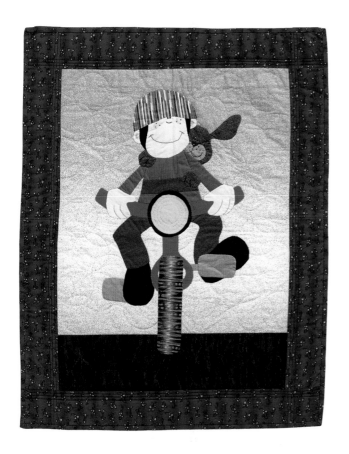

BIKING BUDDIES (BOY) was designed, appliquéd, and quilted by Barbara Roberts, 1995, Catonsville, Maryland, 28" x 35½".

Materials

Note: All measurements are based on 42"-wide fabrics. The fabric colors listed are for your reference and coordinate with the quilt pictured. Feel free to adapt the quilt so that it features your child's favorite colors. All seams are ¼", except binding, which is ⅜". Whenever two fabrics are sewn together by machine (borders to background, sky to ground), press the seam allowance toward the darker fabric.

**The fabric requirements below
are for the girl quilt.**

¾ yd. light blue fabric for sky
¼ yd. green fabric for ground
⅛ yd. each of:
    skin-tone fabric for face and hands
    wild orange fabric for bike helmet
    orange fabric for shirt
    purple fabric for pants
    green fabric for stripe on shirt
    red fabric for bike
    yellow fabric for bike light
    black fabric for shoes and helmet strap
    gray fabric for pedals
    dark gray fabric for bike tire
    brown fabric for dog
    tan fabric for dog's face
    fabric for ponytail
½ yd. dark print for border
⅓ yd. coordinating fabric for binding
1¼ yds. fabric for backing and hanging sleeve
Approximately 30" x 38" piece of batting
Red, blue, black, and brown embroidery floss
Thread to match each fabric

Making the Appliquéd Design

1. From the sky fabric, cut a 21½" x 24" rectangle. From the ground fabric, cut a 5½" x 21½" rectangle. Sew the sky and ground pieces together along their 21½" edges. Press the seam toward the darker fabric.

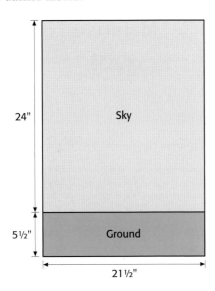

2. Place the pattern found on pages 55–57 on a light box with the background fabric over the pattern. Lightly trace the pattern onto the fabric. Extend the tire lines straight down between the arrows until the total length of the tire is 9".

3. Referring to "Working with Freezer-Paper Templates" on pages 14–17, make freezer-paper templates. Or, refer to "Fusible Appliqué" on pages 22–24 to make your templates from fusible web. Reverse the pattern by flipping it face down on the light box. Trace the entire design. Number each piece. Review the pattern to be sure of where appliqué shapes will overlap one another. Piece #1, the dog's ear, is overlapped by piece #2, the dog's head. Therefore, the fabric around the ear except on the bottom needs to be turned under to give a finished edge. The remaining bottom edge of the ear can be left as a flat edge because it will be overlapped and hidden by piece #2. The paw, piece #9, needs to be basted on all edges. When stitching the paw in place, pin it against piece #6, the sleeve. The 2 pieces should touch so that it appears as though the paw is coming out from under the sleeve.

4. Following the numerical order as indicated in the pattern, stitch or fuse each pattern piece onto the background fabric. Start with piece #1, the dog's ear. Next, appliqué piece #2, the dog's head. If you are making a boy rather than a girl, eliminate appliqué pieces #10 and #18.

5. Embroider facial features with floss or doubled thread. Use the stem stitch for the child's mouth, to outline the fingers, and for the dog's mouth. Use the satin stitch for the child's eyes, and the dog's eyes and nose. To highlight the dog's face, use white thread and add a few stitches on his nose and eyes. Use French knots for freckles. To add dimension to the girl's hair, I used an outline stitch. Use a brown Pigma pen to add small lines on the boy's ears.

Finishing the Quilt

Refer to "Finishing Techniques" on pages 24–30 for additional guidance on finishing your quilt.

1. After the entire top has been appliquéd and embroidered, you're ready to attach the borders. If your appliqué background is oversized, trim it before measuring for borders. The appliquéd portion should measure 21½" x 29". In case your quilt finishes to a different size, check the measurements before cutting borders. (See "Borders" on page 24 for details.) Cut 2 border strips, each 3¾" x 29", and sew them to the sides of the quilt. Press seams toward the borders. Cut 2 strips, each 3¾" x 28", and sew them to the top and bottom of the quilt. Press the seam allowances toward the borders.

2. Cut the batting and backing fabric several inches larger than the top, and pin or baste the 3 layers together.

3. Quilt the layers by hand or machine. Trim the excess batting and backing fabric.

4. Make and attach binding, a hanging sleeve, and a quilt label.

5. As a finishing touch, you can add powdered blush to the child's cheeks and ears.

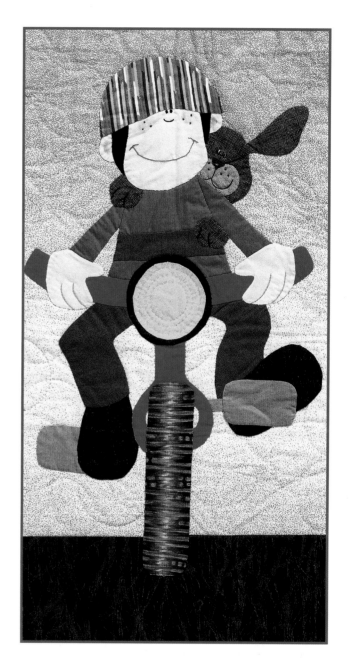

BLAST OFF! was designed, appliquéd, and hand quilted by Barbara Roberts, 1995, Catonsville, Maryland, 25" x 32½".

Blast Off!

Your child can be the star of his or her very own galaxy when you use favorite colors and fabrics to create this space adventurer quilt.

FINISHED QUILT SIZE: 25" x 32½"

Materials

Note: All measurements are based on 42"-wide fabrics. The fabric colors listed are for your reference and coordinate with the quilt pictured. Feel free to adapt the quilt so that it features your child's favorite colors. All seam allowances are ¼", except the binding, which is ⅜".

1½ yds. dark blue print for background, borders, and binding
⅛ yd. red print for narrow border
¼ yd. fabric for top of spaceship (surrounding boy)
¼ yd. white fabric for spaceship
⅛ yd. each of:
    skin-tone fabric for face and hands
    red print for space suit
    black fabric for steering wheel
    red fabric for spaceship decorations and flame
    light gray fabric for spaceship
    dark gray fabric for spaceship
    orange fabric for the flame
    yellow-gold fabric for flame and stars
    brown fabric for dog
    tan fabric for dog's face
1¼ yds. fabric for backing and hanging sleeve
Approximately 30" x 38" piece of batting
Red, blue, black, and brown embroidery floss
Thread to match each fabric
Twelve ½" buttons for spaceship
Three white star buttons for sky

Making the Appliquéd Design

1. From the background fabric, cut a 19½" x 26½" rectangle.

2. Place the pattern found on pages 58–61 on a light box with the background fabric over the pattern. Lightly trace the pattern onto the fabric with a white or light-colored marking pencil so that you'll be able to see the design on the dark background fabric.

3. Referring to "Working with Freezer-Paper Templates" on pages 14–17, make freezer-paper templates. Or, refer to "Fusible Appliqué" on pages 22–24 to make your templates from fusible web. Reverse the pattern by flipping it face down on the light box. Trace the entire design. Number each piece. Review the pattern, and you'll see that piece #1, the orange flame, is overlapped by piece #3, the yellow flame. Therefore, the fabric on the left side of the orange flame needs to be turned under to give a finished edge. The right side of the orange flame is overlapped by the yellow flame and can be left as a flat edge because it won't show. The yellow flame needs to overlap the flat edge of the orange flame to hide it.

4. Stitch or fuse each appliqué piece to the background fabric. Start with piece #1, the orange flame, followed by piece #2, the other orange flame, and continue in numerical order.

5. Embroider the facial features with floss or doubled thread. Use the stem stitch for the boy's mouth, to outline his fingers, for the dog's mouth, and the lines on the spaceship saucer section. Use a satin stitch for the boy's eyes and the dog's eyes and nose. Make French knots for freckles.

Finishing the Quilt

Refer to "Finishing Techniques" on pages 24–30 for additional guidance on finishing your quilt.

1. After the entire top has been appliquéd and embroidered, you're ready to attach the borders. If your appliqué background is oversized, trim it before measuring for borders. The appliquéd portion should measure 19½" x 26½". In case your quilt finishes to a different size, check the measurements before cutting borders. (See "Borders" on page 24 for details.)

2. To make the narrow border, cut 2 strips, each 1" x 26½", and sew them to the sides of the quilt top. Press seams toward the borders. Cut 2 strips, each 1" x 20½", and sew them to the top and bottom of the quilt top. Press seam allowances toward the borders.

3. To give the appearance of continuous sky, the wider borders should be the same fabric as your background fabric. For the wide borders, cut 2 strips, each 2¾" x 27½". Sew them to the sides of the quilt. Cut 2 strips, each 2¾" x 25", and sew them to the top and bottom of the quilt. Press all seam allowances toward the blue borders.

4. Referring to the photograph on page 36 for placement, appliqué a yellow-gold star in each corner of the narrow border.

5. Cut out batting and backing fabric several inches larger than the top and baste the layers together.

6. Quilt the layers by hand or machine, and trim the excess batting and backing fabric.

7. Attach the round buttons to decorate the spaceship and the star buttons in the sky.

8. Make and attach binding, a hanging sleeve, and a quilt label.

9. As a finishing touch, you can add powdered blush for the child's cheeks.

Ice Dancer

Let your little girl follow her dreams of taking center stage on the ice rink with this magical, winter-wonderland creation.

FINISHED QUILT SIZE: 32¾" x 35¾"

Materials

Note: All measurements are based on 42"-wide fabrics. The fabric colors listed are for your reference and coordinate with the quilt pictured. Feel free to adapt the quilt so that it features your child's favorite colors. All seam allowances are ¼", except the binding, which is ⅜".

¾ yd. blue print for sky
¼ yd. light blue print for ice
⅓ yd. or fat quarter of red print for dress
⅛ yd. each of:
    skin-tone fabric for face
    brown fabric for hat
    green fabric for mittens and earmuffs
    white fabric for skates
    dark blue fabric for tights
    3 different gray fabrics for cat
½ yd. dark blue fabric for borders
¼ yd. coordinating fabric for binding
1⅜ yds. fabric for backing and hanging sleeve
Approximately 35" x 38" piece of batting
Red, blue, black, and brown embroidery floss
Thread to match each fabric

Making the Appliquéd Design

1. From the background sky fabric, cut a 20¾" x 25¾" rectangle. From the ice fabric, cut an 8½" x 25¾" rectangle. Sew the pieces together along the 25¾" edge. The finished measurement should be 25¾" x 28¾". Press the seam toward the darker fabric, which in this case is the sky.

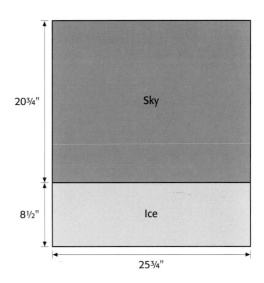

2. Place the pattern found on pages 62–65 on a light box with the background fabric over the pattern. Trace the pattern onto the background fabric.

3. Referring to "Working with Freezer-Paper Templates" on pages 14–17, make freezer-paper templates. Or, refer to "Fusible Appliqué" on pages 22–24 to make your templates from fusible web. Reverse the pattern by flipping it face

ICE DANCER was designed by Barbara Roberts, 1996, Catonsville, Maryland, 32¾" x 35¾". Appliquéd by Barbara Johnson and machine quilted by Ann Brown Christy.

Finishing the Quilt

Refer to "Finishing Techniques" on pages 24-30 for additional guidance on finishing your quilt.

1. After the entire top has been appliquéd and embroidered, you're ready to attach the borders. If you've cut your appliqué background over-sized, trim it before measuring for borders. The appliquéd portion should measure 25¾" x 28¾". In case your quilt finishes to a different size, be sure to check the measurements before cutting borders. (See "Borders" on page 24 for details.) Cut 2 strips, each 4" x 28¾", and sew them to the sides of the quilt. Press seam allowances toward the borders. Cut 2 strips, each 4" x 32¾", and sew them to the top and bottom of the quilt top. Press seams toward the borders.

down on the light box. Trace the entire design. Number each piece. Review the pattern and you'll see that piece #3, her leg, is overlapped by piece #4, her ice skate, and piece #7, her dress. Therefore, you only need to turn under the sides of the leg pieces, not the top and bottom where they'll be overlapped by the dress or skates. You can leave those edges unbasted because they'll be covered and won't show.

4. Following the numerical order as indicated in the pattern, stitch or fuse each piece onto the background fabric. Start with piece #1, the girl's mitten. Next, appliqué piece #2, which is the other mitten. Continue appliquéing in numerical order.

5. Embroider facial features with 2 strands of floss or doubled thread. Use the stem stitch for the skate blades, her nose, and the cat's paws, whiskers, ears, and eyebrows. Use a satin stitch for her eyes, lips, and the cat's eyes and nose. Both the girl and the cat have French knot freckles.

2. Cut the batting and backing fabric several inches larger than the top, and pin or baste the 3 layers together.

3. Quilt the layers by hand or machine, and trim the excess batting and backing fabric.

4. Make and attach binding, a hanging sleeve, and a quilt label.

5. As a finishing touch, you can add powdered blush to the girl's cheeks.

LOOK MA, NO HANDS (GIRL) was designed and appliquéd by Barbara Roberts, 1999, Catonsville, Maryland, 26" x 32¾". Machine quilted by Ann Brown Christy.

Look Ma, No Hands

Soccer is such a popular sport today that every family is bound to have at least one budding all-star. Show your favorite player that you're his or her biggest fan with a personalized soccer quilt.

FINISHED QUILT SIZE: 26" x 32¾"

LOOK MA, NO HANDS (BOY) was designed by Barbara Roberts, 1999, Catonsville, Maryland, 26" x 32¾". Appliquéd by Helen Quane and machine quilted by Ann Brown Christy.

Materials

Note: All measurements are based on 42"-wide fabrics. The fabric colors listed are for your reference and coordinate with the quilt pictured. Feel free to adapt the quilt so that it features your child's favorite colors. All seam allowances are ¼", except the binding, which is ⅜".

The fabric requirements below are for the girl quilt.

½ yd. blue fabric for sky

⅝ yd. green fabric for grass

⅛ yd. or fat quarter of pink fabric for shirt and cuffs on socks

⅛ yd. each of:
    skin-tone fabric for face, hands, and legs
    pink fabric for socks
    fabric for hair
    yellow fabric for shorts
    black print fabric for shoes
    3 gray prints for shoes (3 different values: light, medium, dark)

6" x 6" square *each* of black and white fabrics for soccer ball

¼ yd. fabric for borders

¼ yd. coordinating fabric for binding

1¼ yds. fabric for backing and hanging sleeve

Approximately 28" x 35" piece of batting

Red, black, and brown embroidery floss

Thread to match each fabric

Making the Appliquéd Design

1. From the blue background fabric, cut an 11½" x 18½" rectangle. From the green background fabric, cut a 14½" x 18½" rectangle. Sew the 2 rectangles together along their 18½" edges. Press seams toward the darker fabric.

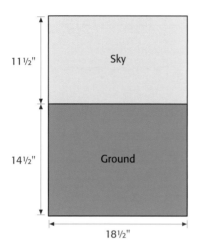

2. Place the pattern found on pages 66–70 on a light box with the background fabric over the pattern. Trace the pattern onto the fabric. The girl is drawn on the pattern facing toward the left. If you want her or a boy facing toward the right, you'll need to reverse all directional instructions.

3. Referring to "Working with Freezer-Paper Templates" on pages 14–17, make freezer-paper templates. Or, refer to "Fusible Appliqué" on pages 22–24 to make your templates from fusible web. Reverse the pattern by flipping it face down on the light box. Trace the entire design. Number each piece. Review the pattern and you'll see piece #26 (the ponytail) is overlapped by piece #27 (the back of her head). Therefore, the ponytail fabric needs to be basted under on all edges except the edge that will be overlapped by piece #27. That edge can be left unbasted or flat because it will be under the head and won't show. Of course, if you are making a boy, omit piece #26, the ponytail.

4. Following the numerical order as indicated in the pattern, sew or fuse each appliqué onto the background fabric, starting with piece #1, the back leg. Next attach piece #2, the knee, and continue appliquéing in numerical order.

5. Embroider facial features with 2 strands of floss or doubled thread. Use a stem stitch for the mouth and nose and to outline the fingers and ear. Fill in the eyes with a satin stitch. Make French knot freckles to complete the face.

Finishing the Quilt

Refer to "Finishing Techniques" on pages 24–30 for additional guidance on finishing your quilt.

1. After the entire top has been appliquéd and embroidered, you're ready to attach the borders. If you've cut your appliqué background over-sized, trim it before measuring for borders. The appliquéd portion should measure 18½" x 25¼". In case your quilt finishes to a different size, be sure to check the measurements before cutting borders. (See "Borders" on page 24 for details.) Cut 2 border strips, each 4¼" x 18½", and sew them to the top and bottom of the quilt top. Press seam allowances toward the borders. Cut 2 strips, each 4¼" x 32¾", and sew them to the sides of the quilt. Press seams toward the borders.

2. After the borders are sewn on, the soccer ball is added. To make the soccer ball, I used reverse appliqué. See "Making a Reverse Appliqué Soccer Ball" below.

3. Cut the batting and backing fabric several inches larger than the top, and pin or baste the 3 layers together.

4. Quilt the layers by hand or machine, and trim the excess batting and backing fabric.

5. Make and attach binding, a hanging sleeve, and a quilt label.

6. As a finishing touch, you can add powdered blush to the child's cheeks.

Making a Reverse Appliqué Soccer Ball

Instead of sewing one fabric onto the top of another as in appliqué, you start out with two or more fabrics pinned together and cut the top layer away revealing the other fabric below. For the soccer ball you need two fabrics, one black and one white.

1. Cut a 6" x 6" square of each fabric.

2. Place the white fabric right side up over the illustration in the book, and trace all the lines of the soccer ball. I used a permanent Pigma pen, black with a .01 tip. You can use a mechanical pencil with a light touch if you prefer.

3. Place an **X** in the middle of each area of the ball which will be cut away to reveal the black. With your fabric scissors cut a *small* slit through the **X** in each white area. Slitting the fabric before pinning it to the black fabric makes it easier to cut away the fabric once the two pieces are pinned together.

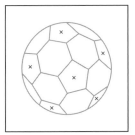

Mark areas to be cut away with an ✕.

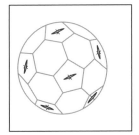

Cut a slit through each ✕.

4. Pin the white fabric over the black fabric, both with right sides facing you. Pin around the soccer ball as well as inside each white area that is large enough to accommodate a sequin pin.

Black fabric underneath

5. Starting with the black area in the middle of the ball, cut away the white fabric in that area. Start in the center and snip toward each corner, stopping one thread short of the point where the lines meet.

6. Cut the white fabric so that only a scant ¼" seam allowance remains.

7. Thread your needle with black thread. Tie a knot in the end and put the needle into the fabric from the back. Come up at any corner of the trimmed area. Take 2 small stitches into the corner to catch any threads that might fray from this point.

8. With the tip of your needle, turn the edge of the white fabric under the white fabric so that the black fabric shows through. Stitch completely around the edge of the area, turning all the white fabric under so that only the black area remains.

9. Repeat steps 5–8 on pages 45–46 for each white area that is marked with an X.

10. When all the black parts of the ball have been revealed, cut out the ball. Leave a ¼" seam allowance around the outside edge.

11. Pin the ball to the quilt so it overlaps the border and the grass, as indicated on the pattern.

12. Turning the edge of the ball under with your needle, sew the ball to the quilt. If you prefer to use freezer paper, make a template for the soccer ball and baste the edges to the freezer paper as you did for other shapes in the quilt.

13. Embroider black lines on the ball to indicate the individual white hexagons. Or, use a Pigma pen to draw the lines.

Fusing the Soccer Ball

If you use fusible appliqué for your project, make the soccer ball by making a fusible-web template of the entire soccer ball and pressing it onto the white fabric. Make individual fusible-web templates for each of the black areas. Fuse the black pentagons onto the white soccer ball. Cut out the ball and fuse it in place on the quilt top so it overlaps the background and border, as shown on the pattern.

Rolling Along

Active kids love the freedom they feel when slipping into a pair of in-line skates. They're sure to love starring in this special quilt.

FINISHED QUILT SIZE: 22½" x 33¼"

ROLLING ALONG (GIRL) was designed and appliquéd by Barbara Roberts, 1996, Catonsville, Maryland, 22½" x 33¼". Machine quilted by Ann Brown Christy.

Materials

Note: All measurements are based on 42"-wide fabrics. The fabric colors listed are for your reference and coordinate with the quilt pictured. Feel free to adapt the quilt so that it features your child's favorite colors. All seam allowances are ¼", except the binding, which is ⅜".

The fabric requirements below are for the boy quilt.

½ yd. fabric for sky

¼ yd. print for shirt

⅛ yd. each of:

    skin-tone fabric for face, arms, and legs

    black print for the helmet, skates, and elbow and knee pads

    orange print for the helmet and skates

    purple print for the shorts

    fabric for hair

    dark orange strip for skates

⅓ yd. fabric for wide border

⅛ yd. fabric for narrow border

¼ yd. coordinating fabric for binding

1 yd. fabric for backing and hanging sleeve

Approximately 24" x 35" piece of batting

Blue, red, black, and brown embroidery floss

Thread to match each fabric

ROLLING ALONG (BOY) was designed by Barbara Roberts, 1999, Catonsville, Maryland, 22" x 32¾". Appliquéd by Diana L. Harper and machine quilted by Ann Brown Christy.

Making the Appliquéd Design

1. From the background fabric, cut a 16" x 26¾" rectangle.

2. Place the pattern found on pages 71–74 on a light box with the background fabric over the pattern. Trace the pattern onto the fabric.

3. Referring to "Working with Freezer-Paper Templates" on pages 14–17, make freezer-paper templates. Or, refer to "Fusible Appliqué" on pages 22–24 to make your templates from fusible web. Reverse the pattern by flipping it face down on the light box. Trace the entire design. Number each piece. If you are making the girl quilt, note that piece #24, the ponytail, is overlapped by piece #33, her helmet, and piece #25, the back of her head. Therefore, the ponytail fabric needs to be turned under on all edges except the edge that will be overlapped by pieces #33 and #25. That edge can be left unbasted because it will be covered by other pieces and won't show.

4. Following the numerical order as indicated in the pattern, stitch or fuse each appliqué onto the background fabric, starting with piece #1, a wheel. Next, stitch piece #2, the next wheel, followed by piece #3 and so on. Note that if you are making a girl, you will need appliqué piece #24, the ponytail.

5. Embroider facial features with 2 strands of floss or doubled thread. Use a stem stitch for the mouth and nose and to outline the fingers and ear. Fill in the eyes with a satin stitch. Finish the face details with French-knot freckles. I used a brown Pigma pen to outline the outstretched hand.

Finishing the Quilt

Refer to "Finishing Techniques" on pages 24–30 for additional guidance on finishing your quilt.

1. After the entire top has been appliquéd and embroidered, you're ready to attach the borders.

If your appliqué background is oversized, trim it before measuring for borders. The appliquéd portion should measure 16" x 26¾". In case your quilt finishes to a different size, be sure to check the measurements before cutting borders. (See "Borders" on page 24 for details.)

2. To make the narrow borders, cut 2 strips, each 1" x 16", and sew them to the top and bottom of the quilt top; press seams toward the borders. Cut 2 strips, each 1" x 27¾", and sew them to each side of the quilt top; press seams toward the borders.

3. For the wider borders, cut 2 strips, each 3¼" x 17", and sew them to the top and bottom of the quilt top; press seams toward the wide borders. Cut 2 strips, each 3¼" x 33¼", and sew them to the sides of the quilt top; press seams toward the wide borders.

4. Cut the batting and backing fabric several inches larger than the top, and pin or baste the 3 layers together.

5. Quilt the layers by hand or machine, and trim the excess batting and backing fabric.

6. Make and attach binding, a hanging sleeve, and a quilt label.

7. As a finishing touch, you can add powdered blush to the child's cheeks.

WHOOSH (GIRL) was designed and appliquéd by Barbara Roberts, 1996, Catonsville, Maryland, 28½" x 35". Machine quilted by Ann Brown Christy.

Whoosh

Skateboarding offers great fun—and freedom from gravity! This adventurous child soars high above the ground, and taking kitty along for the ride makes it even more exciting.

FINISHED QUILT SIZE: 28½" x 35"

WHOOSH (BOY) was designed by Barbara Roberts, 1999, Catonsville, Maryland, 28½" x 35". Appliquéd by Elisabeth J. Rollman and machine quilted by Ann Brown Christy.

Materials

Note: All measurements are based on 42"-wide fabrics. The fabric colors listed are for your reference and coordinate with the quilt pictured. Feel free to adapt the quilt so that it features your child's favorite colors. All seam allowances are ¼", except the binding, which is ⅜".

The fabric requirements below are for the girl quilt.

⅔ yd. print fabric for sky

⅓ yd. or fat quarter of red print for shirt

¼ yd. colorful fabric for skateboard

⅛ yd. each of:

    skin-tone fabric for face and hands

    medium purple fabric for pants

    dark purple fabric for pants

    white fabric for sneakers

    black fabric for soles of sneakers and sides
       of wheels

    medium gray fabric for wheels

    light gray fabric for axles

    fabric for hair

    cream fabric for cat

    tan fabric for cat's face

½ yd. fabric for borders

¼ yd. coordinating fabric for binding

1⅜ yds. fabric for backing and hanging sleeve

Approximately 30" x 36" piece of batting

Red, black, and brown embroidery floss

Thread to match each fabric

Making the Appliquéd Design

1. From the background fabric, cut a 21" x 27½" rectangle.

2. Place the pattern found on pages 75–79 on a light box with the background fabric over the pattern. Trace the pattern onto the fabric.

3. Referring to "Working with Freezer-Paper Templates" on pages 14–17, make freezer-paper templates. Or, refer to "Fusible Appliqué" on pages 22–24 to make your templates from fusible web. Reverse the pattern by flipping it face down on the light box. Trace the entire design. Number each piece. Review the pattern and you'll see that piece #1, the ponytail, is overlapped by piece #2, her hair. Therefore, the ponytail fabric needs to be turned under on all edges except where it is overlapped by the back of her head. Where the ponytail will be overlapped, it can be left unbasted or flat because it will be covered by piece #2.

4. Following the numerical order on the pattern, stitch or fuse each pattern piece onto the background fabric. Start with piece #1, the girl's ponytail. Next, appliqué piece #2, the hair, and continue in order. If you are making a boy rather than a girl, eliminate piece #1, the ponytail.

5. Embroider facial features with 2 strands of floss or doubled thread. Use the stem stitch for the child's mouth and nose and to outline the fingers and ear. Use a stem stitch to embroider the cat's mouth, eyebrows, and line between the legs. For the child's eyes and the cat's nose and eyes, use a satin stitch. Finish the face details with French knot freckles.

Finishing the Quilt

Refer to "Finishing Techniques" on pages 24–30 for additional guidance on finishing your quilt.

1. After the entire top has been appliquéd and embroidered, you're ready to attach the borders. If your appliqué background is oversized, trim it before measuring for borders. The appliquéd portion should measure 21" x 27½". In case your quilt finishes to a different size, be sure to check the measurements before cutting borders. (See "Borders" on page 24 for details.) Cut 2 strips, each 4¼" x 21", and sew these border strips to the top and bottom of the quilt. (If your fabric is at least 42" wide, you can cut 1 strip 4¼" wide, and cut this strip into 2 lengths that measure 21" x 4¼".) Press seam allowances toward the borders. Cut 2 strips, each 4¼" x 35", and sew these to the sides of the quilt. Press seams toward the borders.

2. Cut the batting and backing fabric several inches larger than the top, and pin or baste the 3 layers together.

3. Quilt the layers by hand or machine, and trim the excess batting and backing fabric.

4. Make and attach binding, a hanging sleeve, and a quilt label.

5. As a finishing touch, you can add powdered blush to the child's cheeks.

53

Patterns

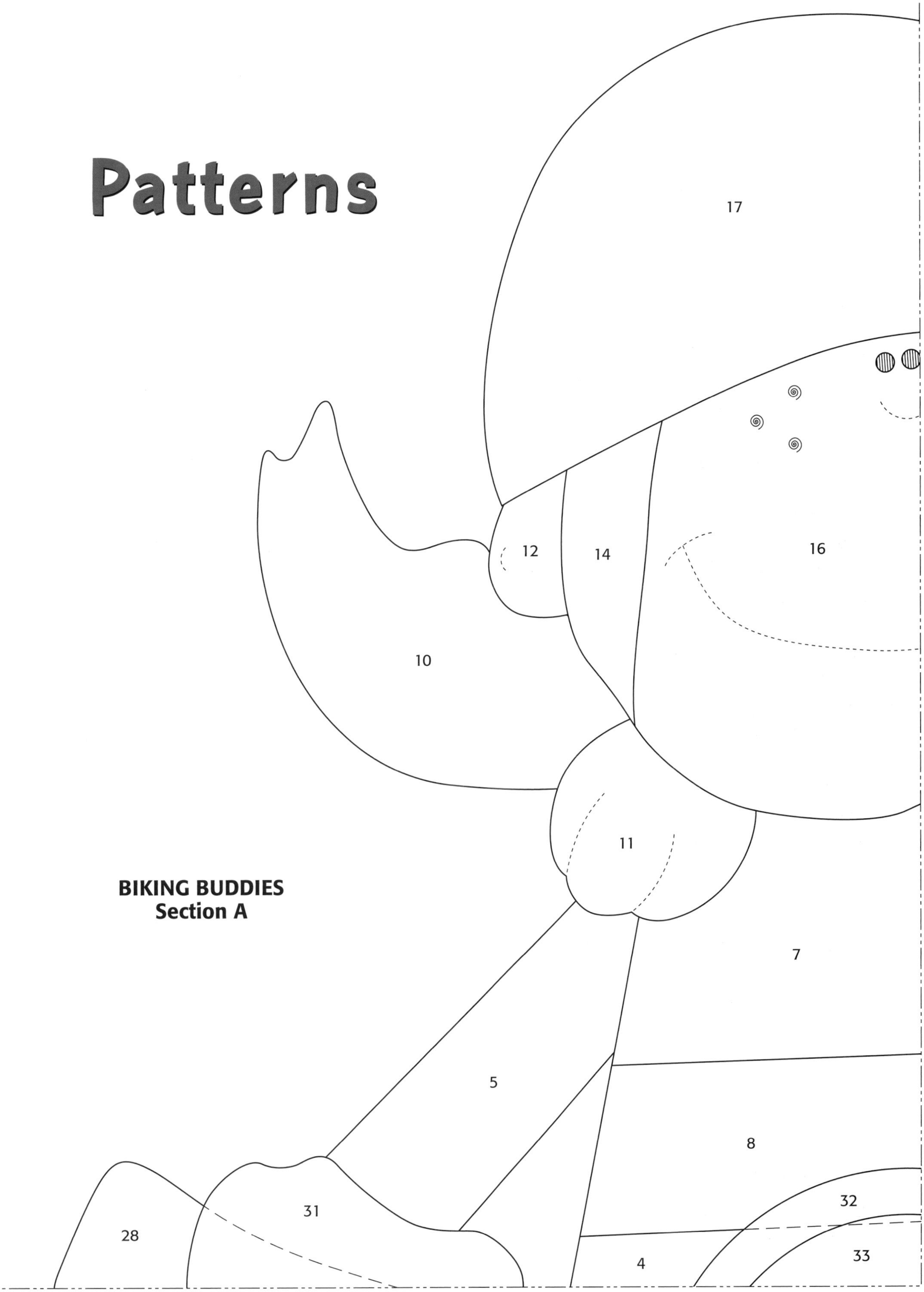

17

12 14

16

10

11

BIKING BUDDIES
Section A

7

5

8

28 31 32

4 33

BIKING BUDDIES
Section B

18

15   13

2

3

1

6

9

30

29

4

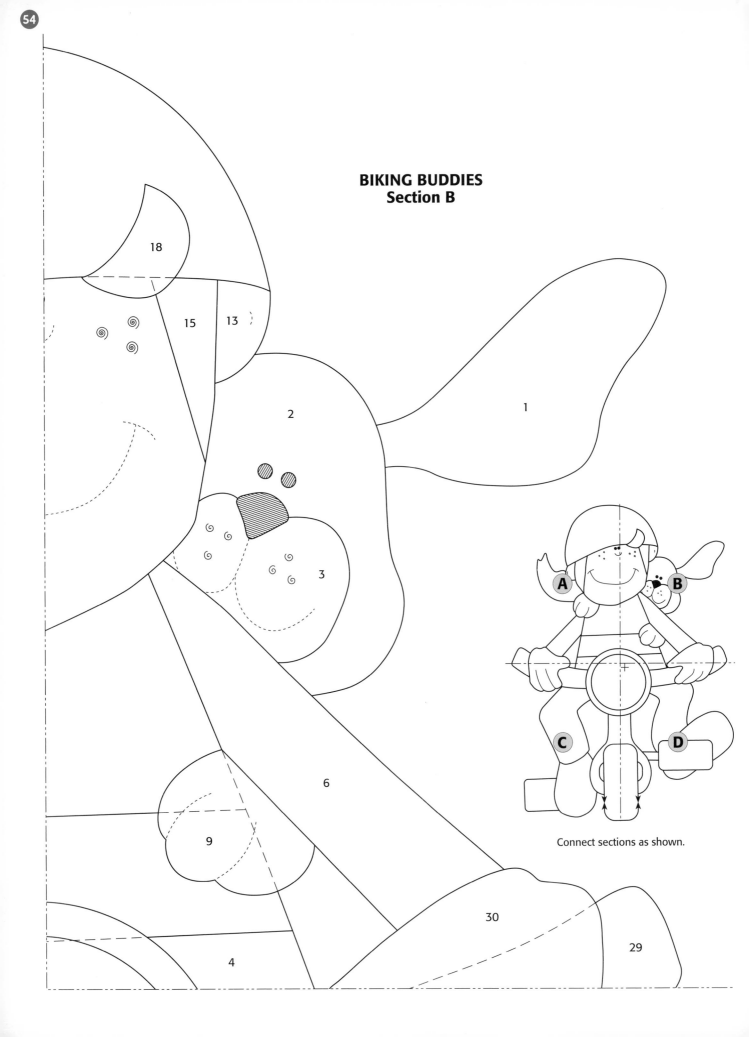

Connect sections as shown.

A   B

C   D

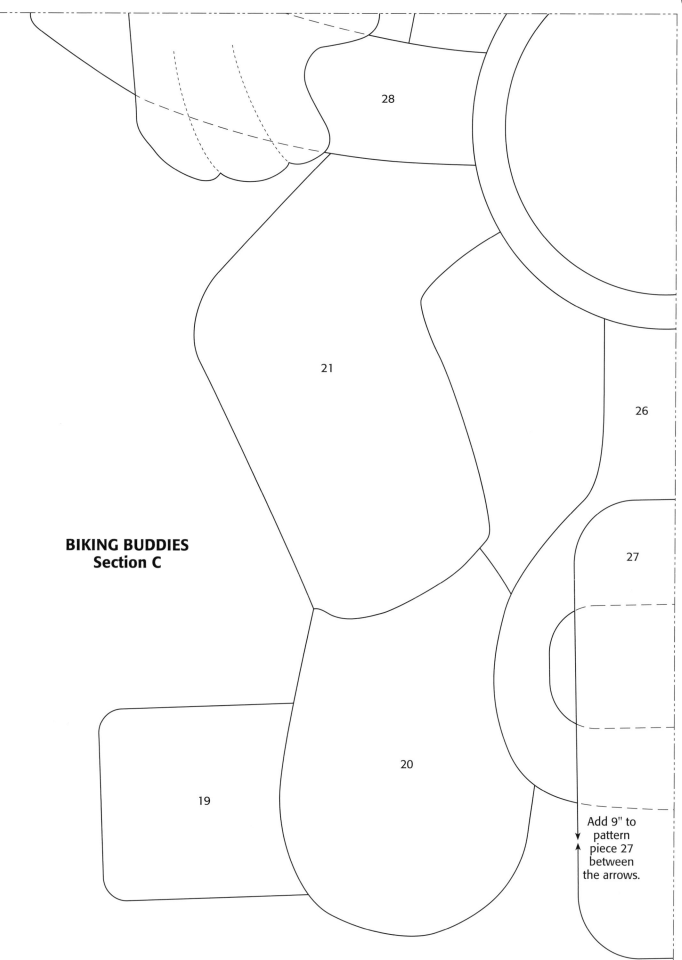

BIKING BUDDIES
Section C

28

21

26

27

20

19

Add 9" to
pattern
piece 27
between
the arrows.

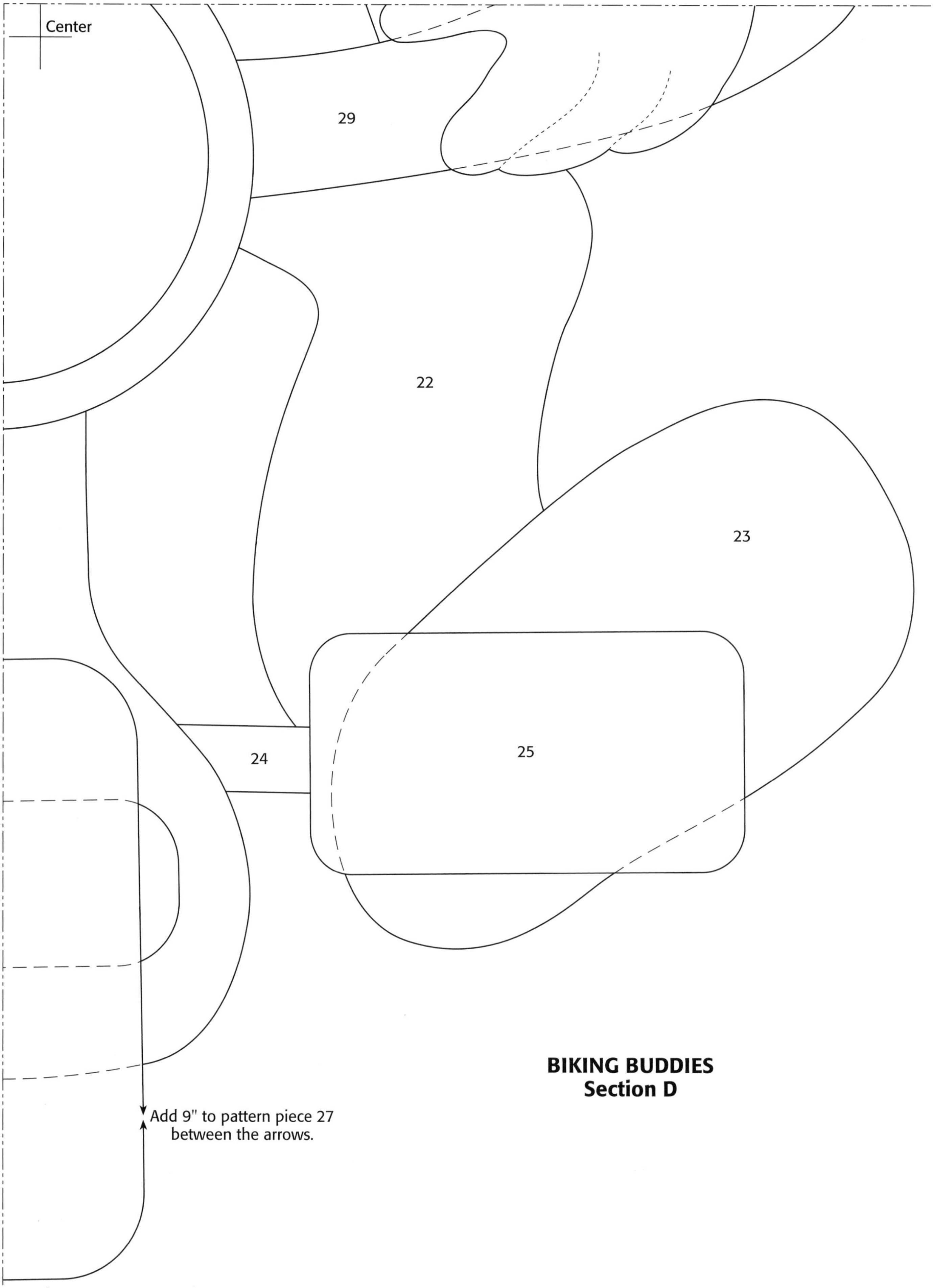

Center

29

22

23

24

25

**BIKING BUDDIES
Section D**

Add 9" to pattern piece 27
between the arrows.

BLAST OFF!
Section A

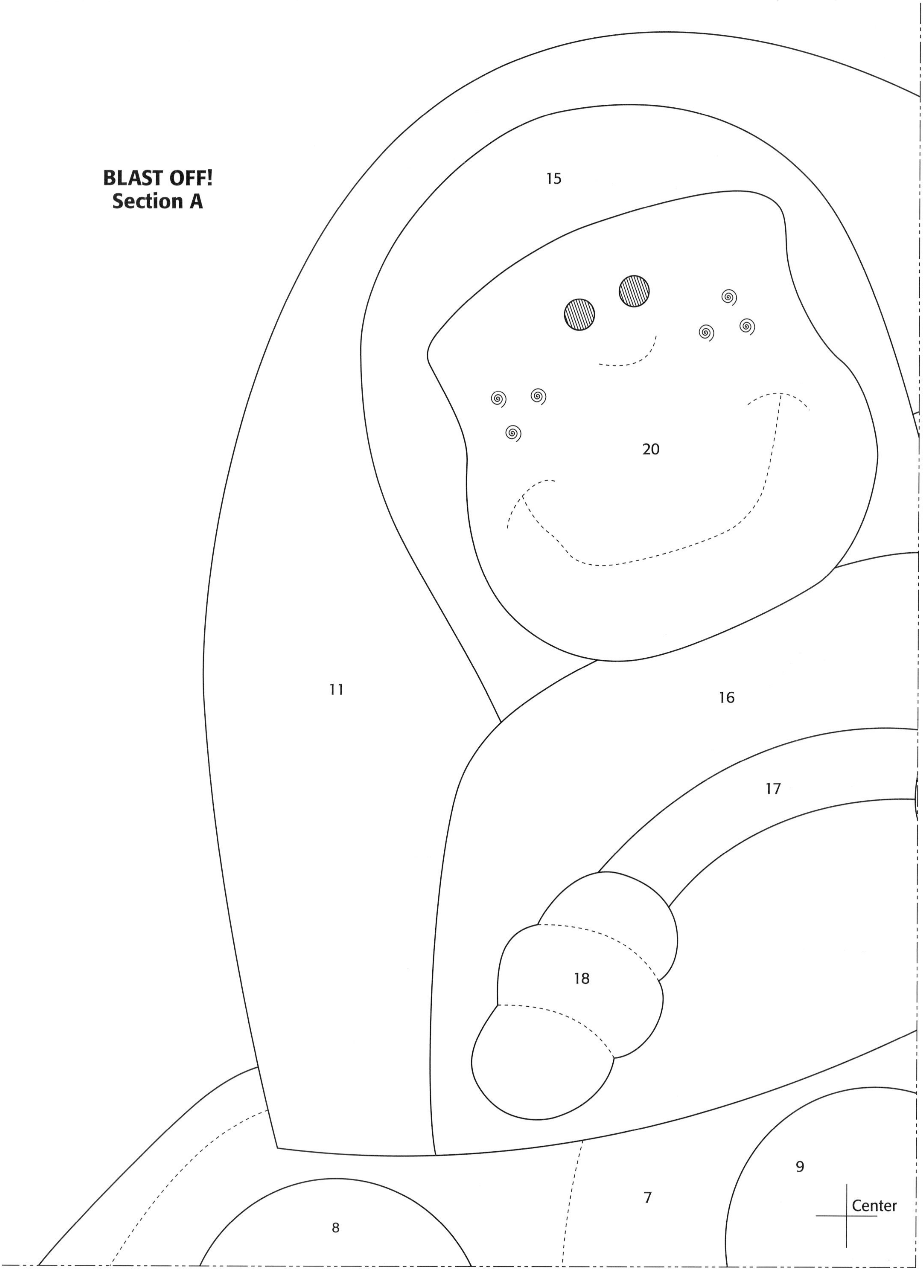

15

20

11

16

17

18

7

9

8

Center

BLAST OFF!
Section B

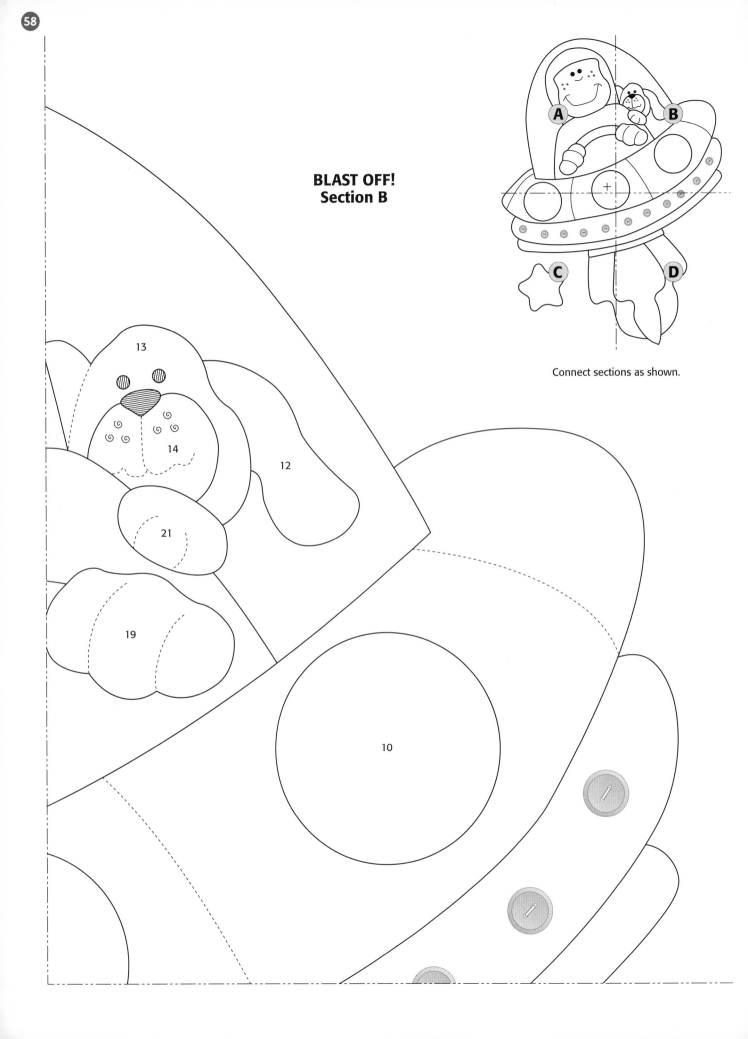

Connect sections as shown.

13

14

12

21

19

10

6

5

4

Cut 4

1

BLAST OFF!
Section C

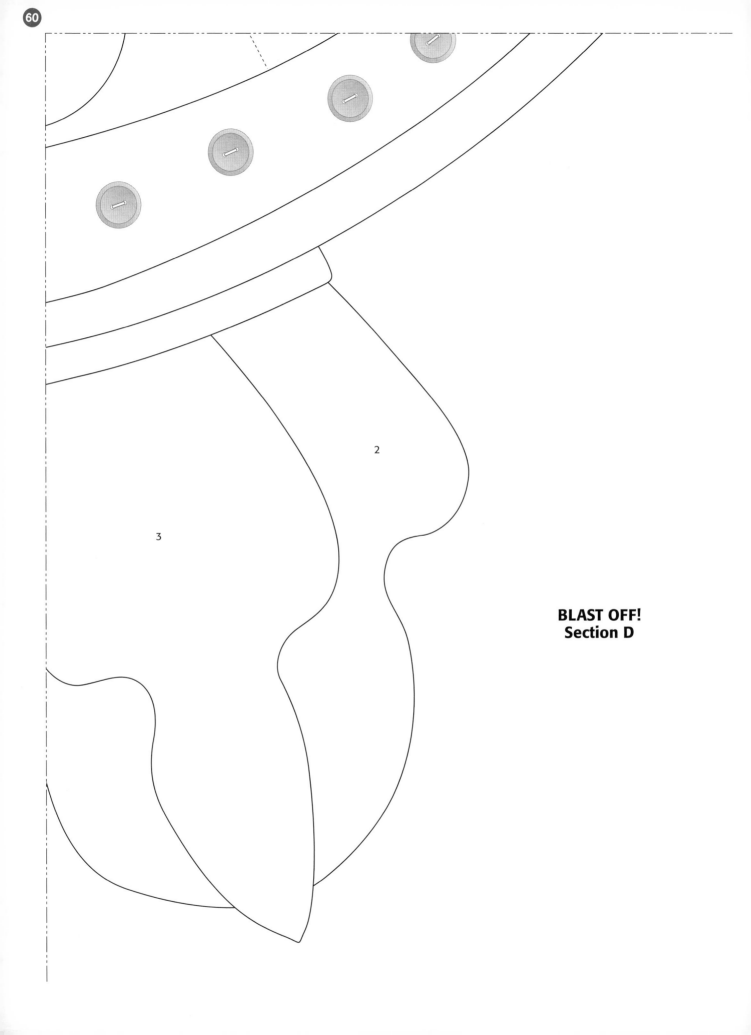

BLAST OFF!
Section D

2

3

**ICE DANCER
Section A**

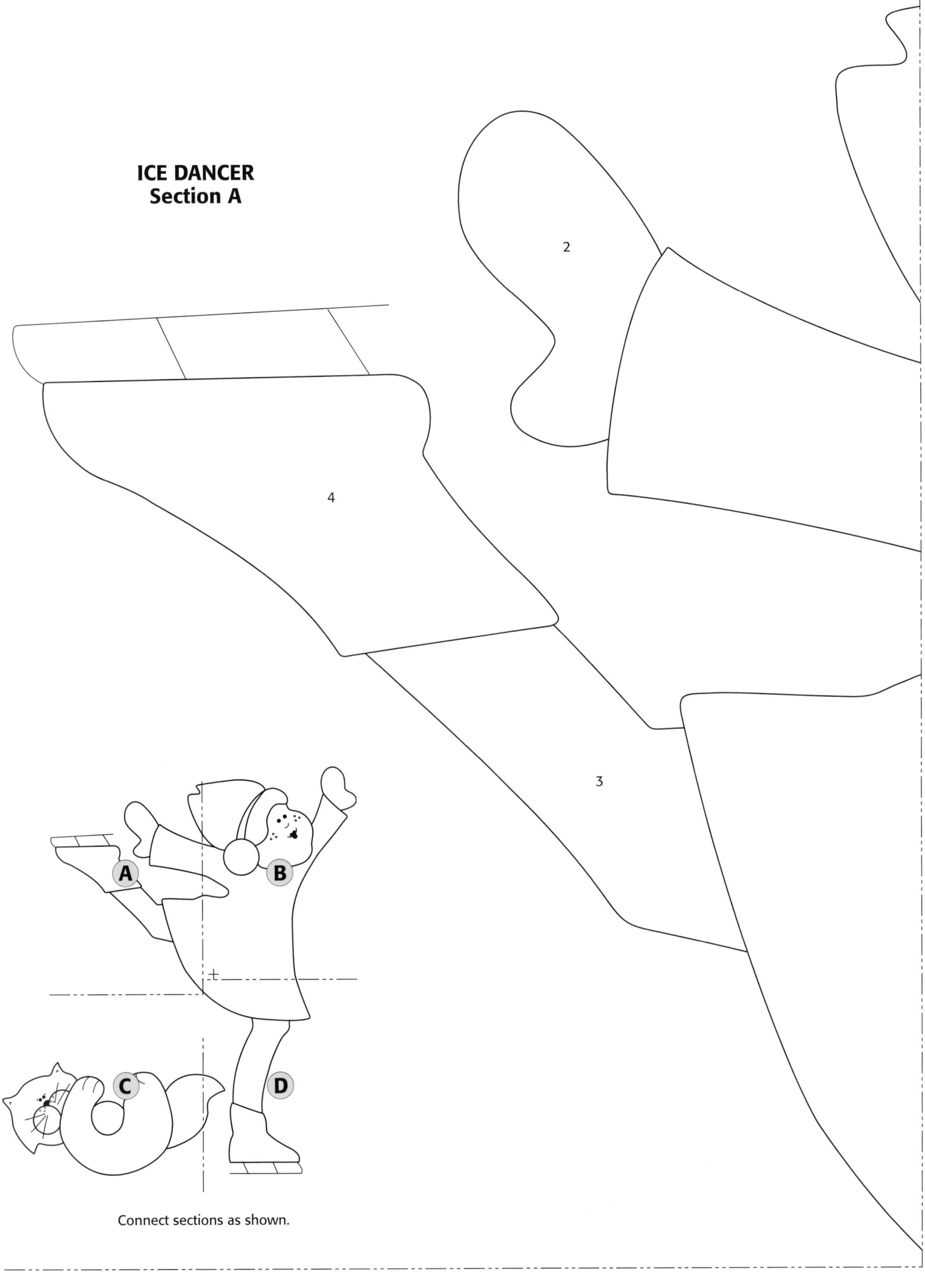

2

4

3

A

B

C

D

Connect sections as shown.

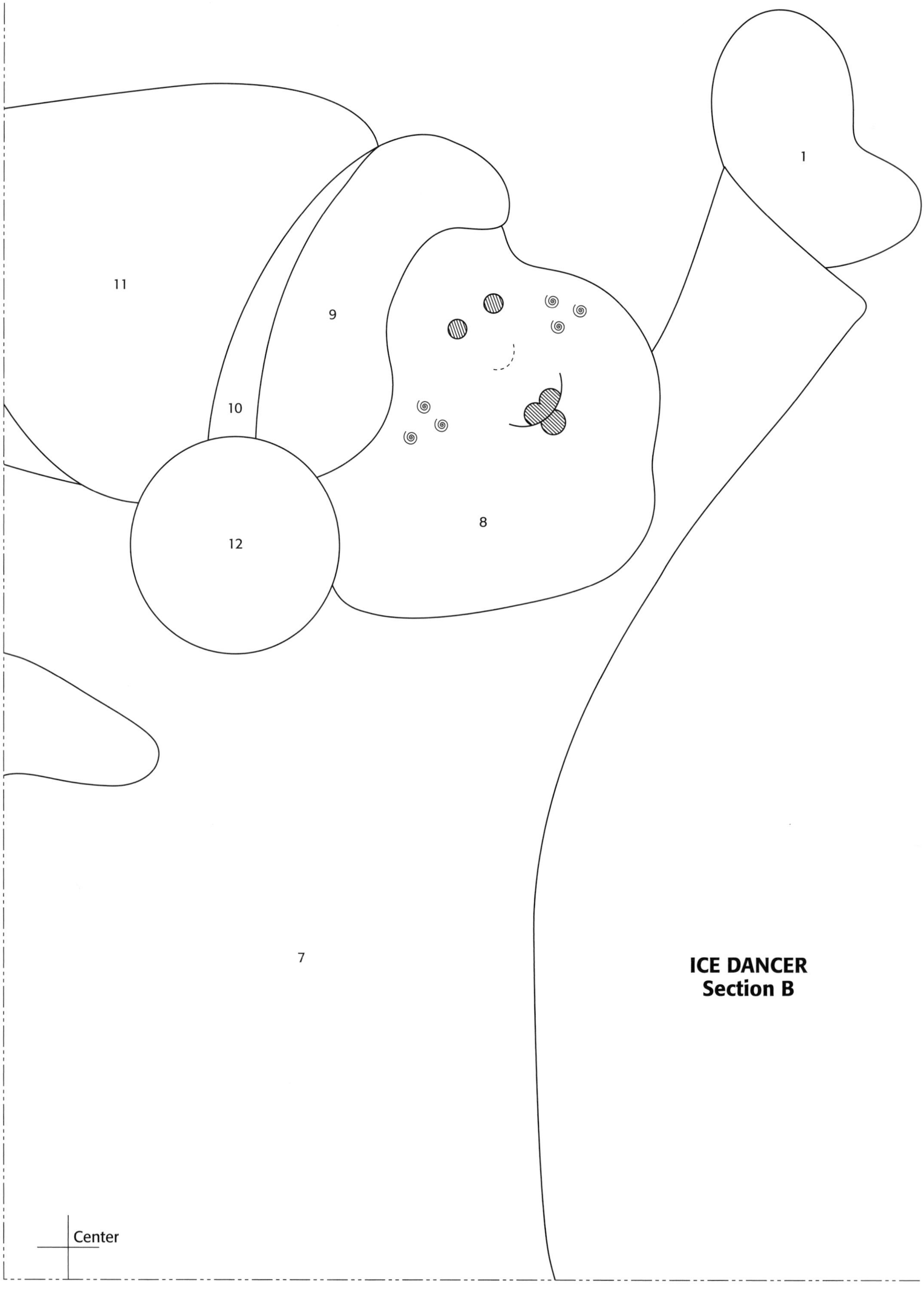

1

11

9

10

12

8

7

**ICE DANCER
Section B**

Center

ICE DANCER
Section C

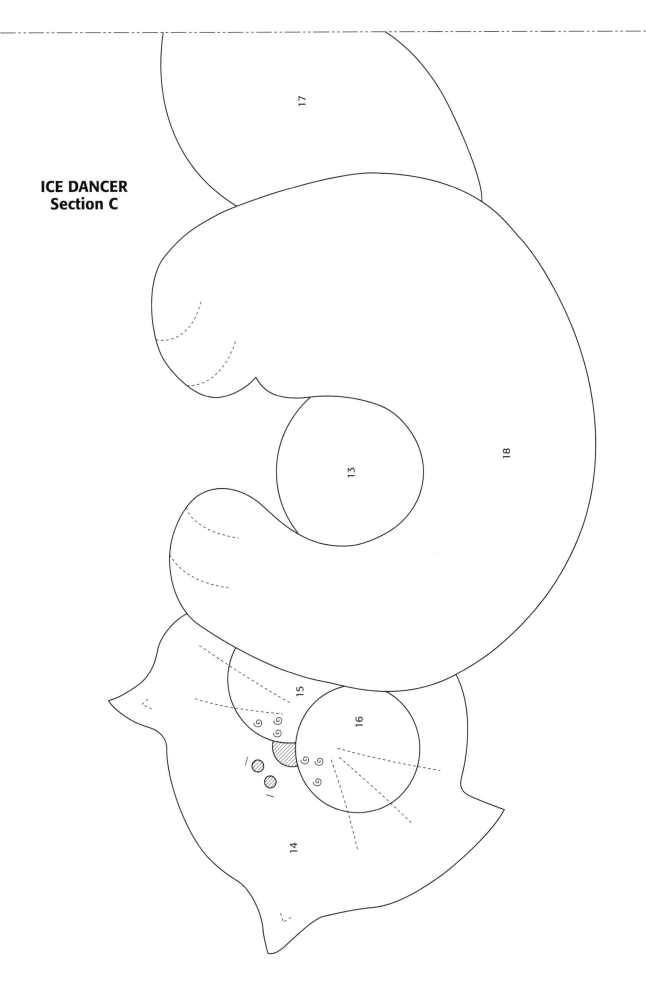

64

5

**ICE DANCER
Section D**

6

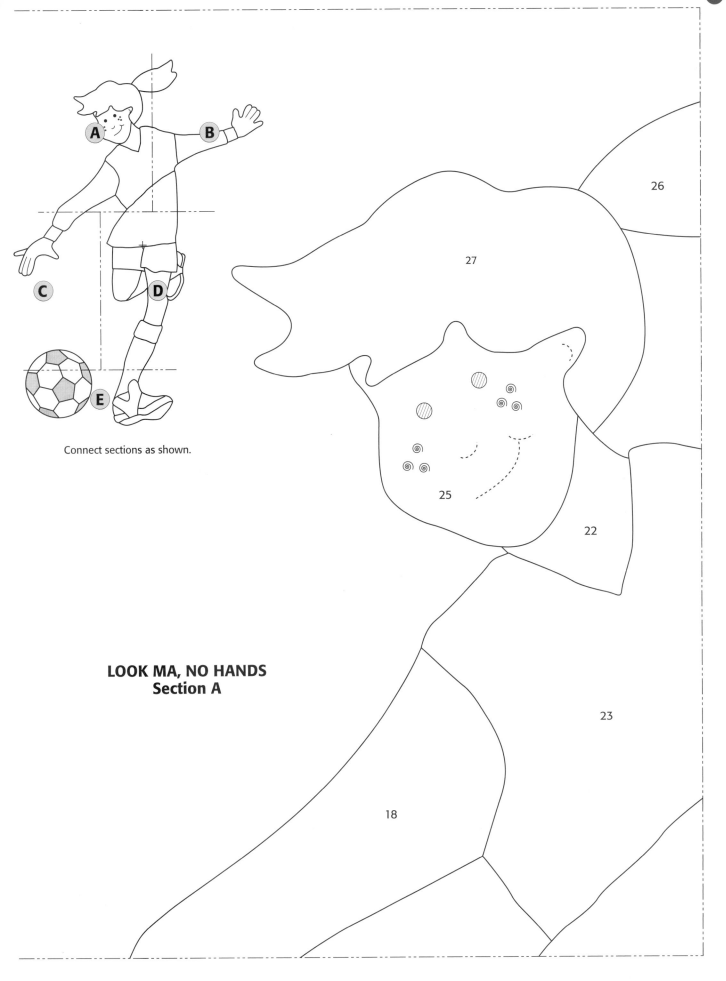

Connect sections as shown.

LOOK MA, NO HANDS
Section A

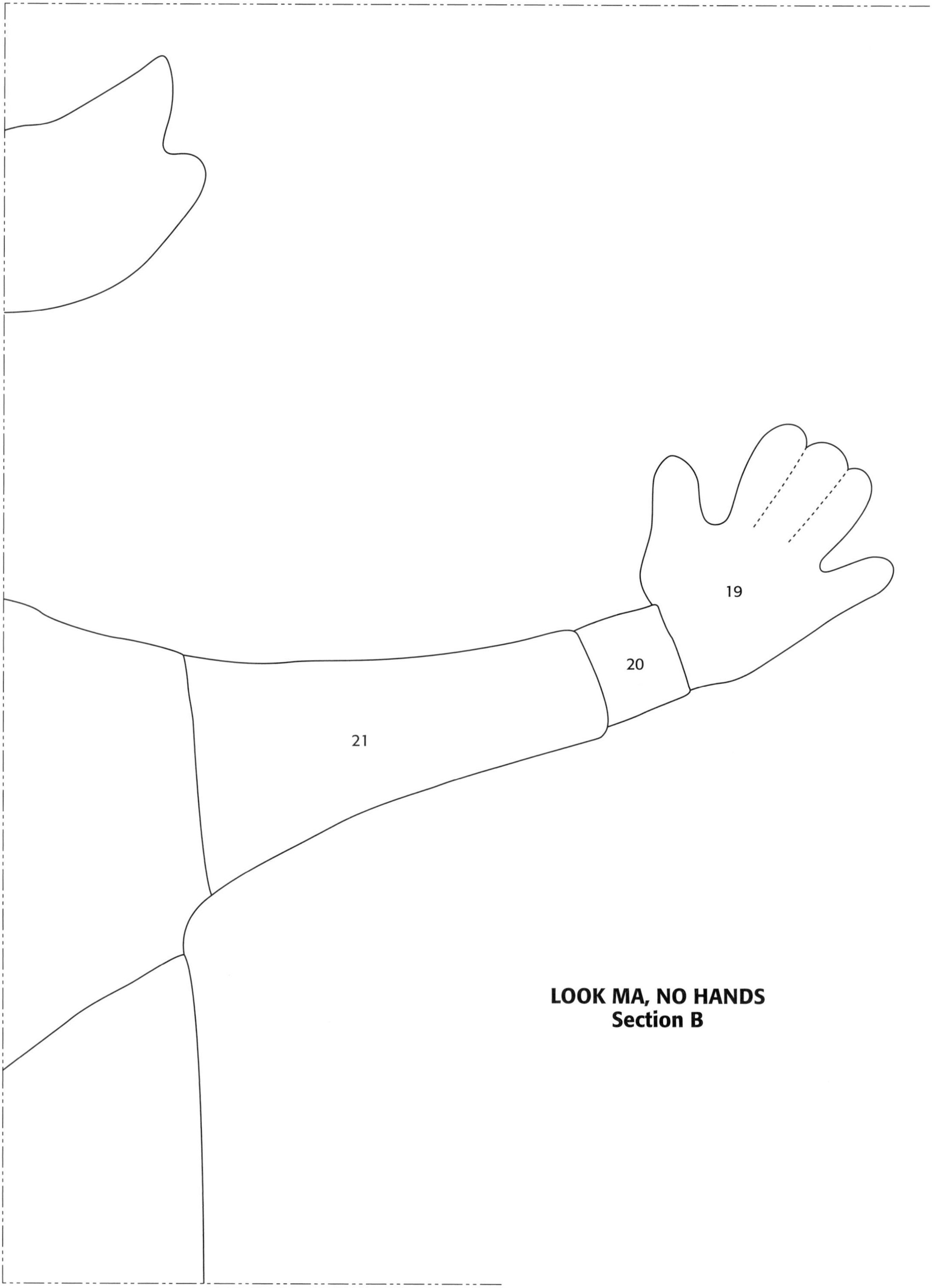

19

20

21

LOOK MA, NO HANDS
Section B

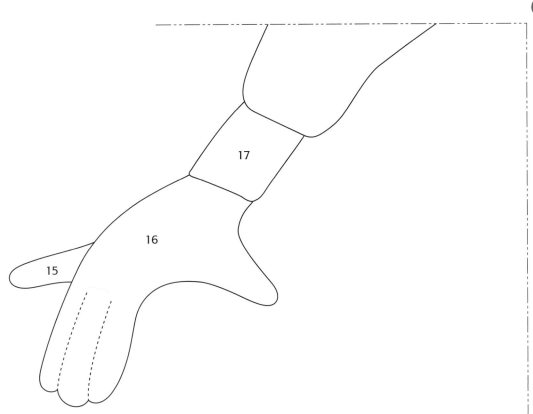

15
16
17

LOOK MA, NO HANDS
Section C

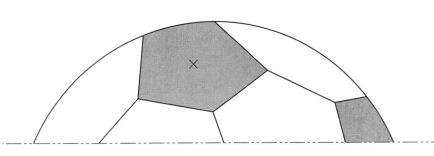

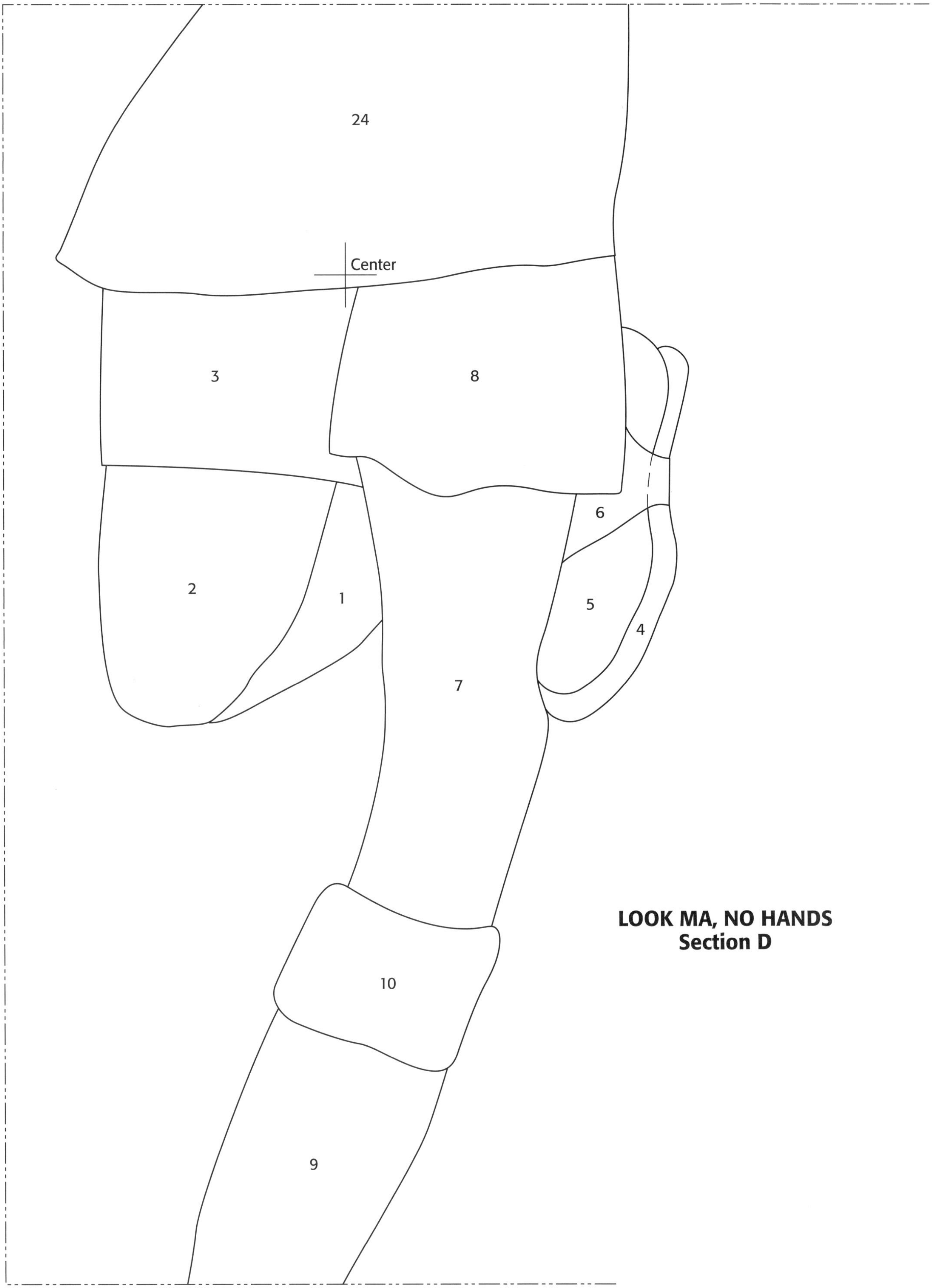

24

Center

3

8

2

1

6

5

4

7

LOOK MA, NO HANDS
Section D

10

9

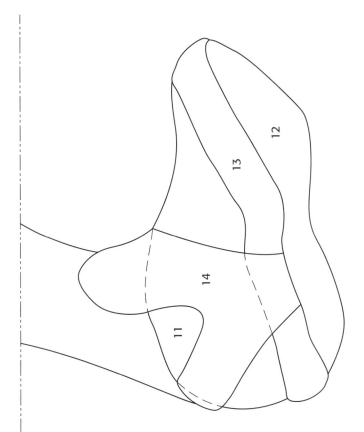

LOOK MA, NO HANDS
Section E

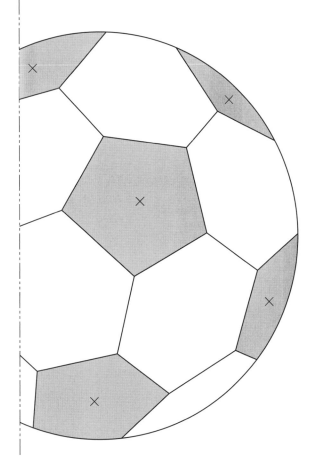

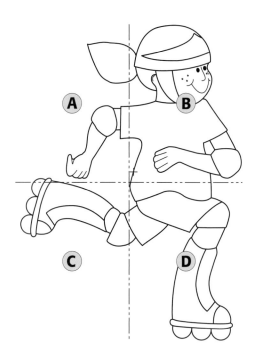

Connect sections as shown.

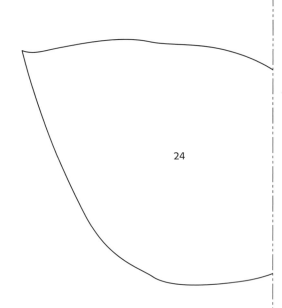

24

ROLLING ALONG
Section A

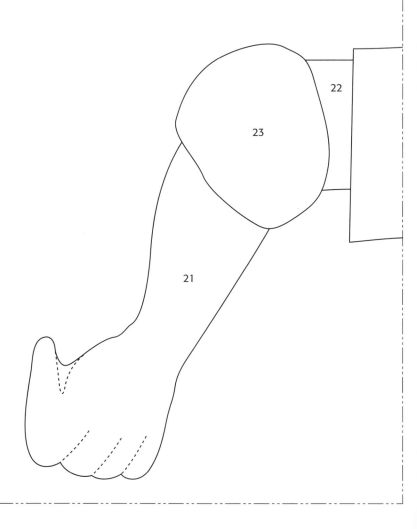

22

23

21

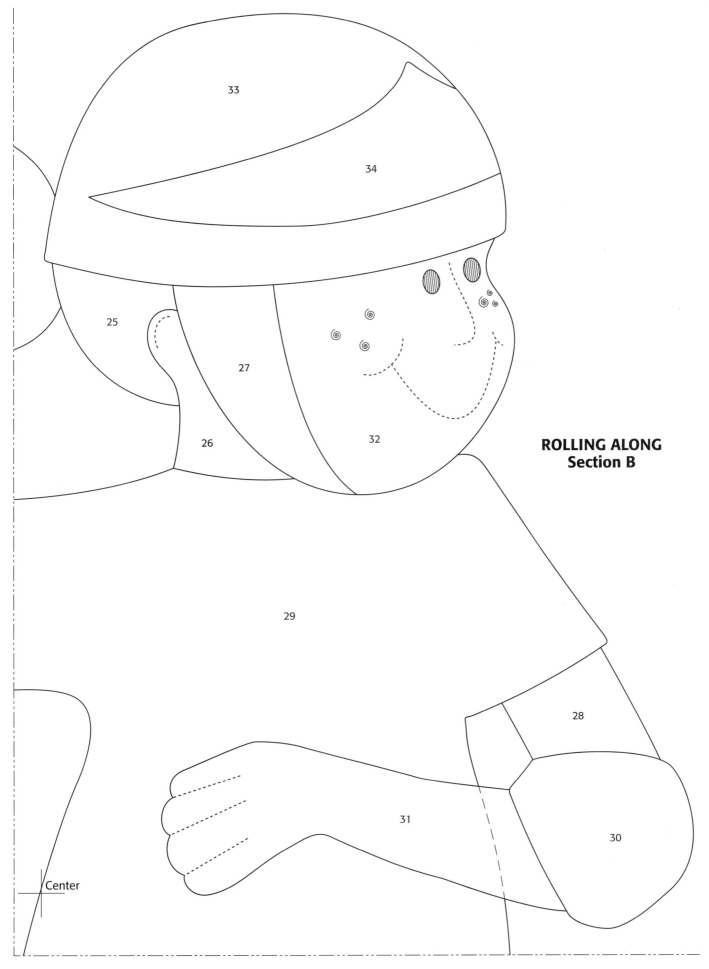

**ROLLING ALONG
Section B**

Center

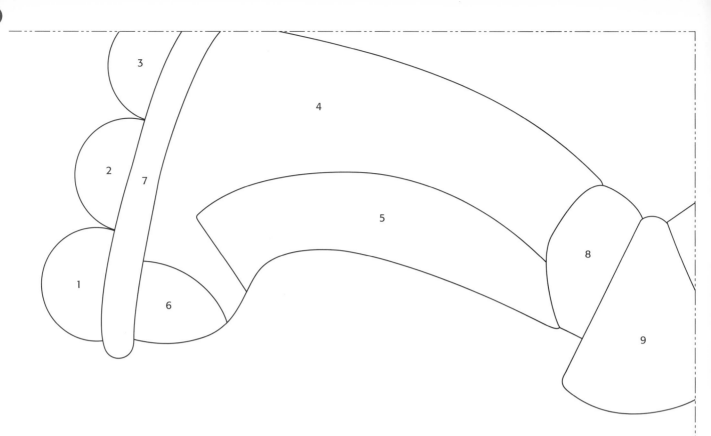

ROLLING ALONG
Section C

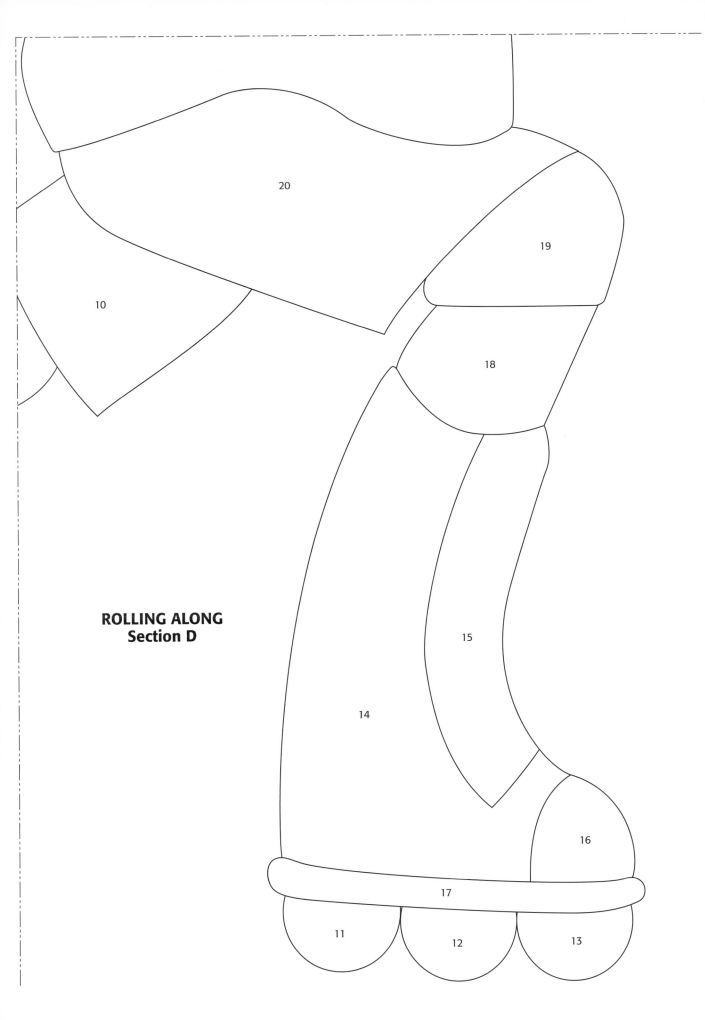

ROLLING ALONG
Section D

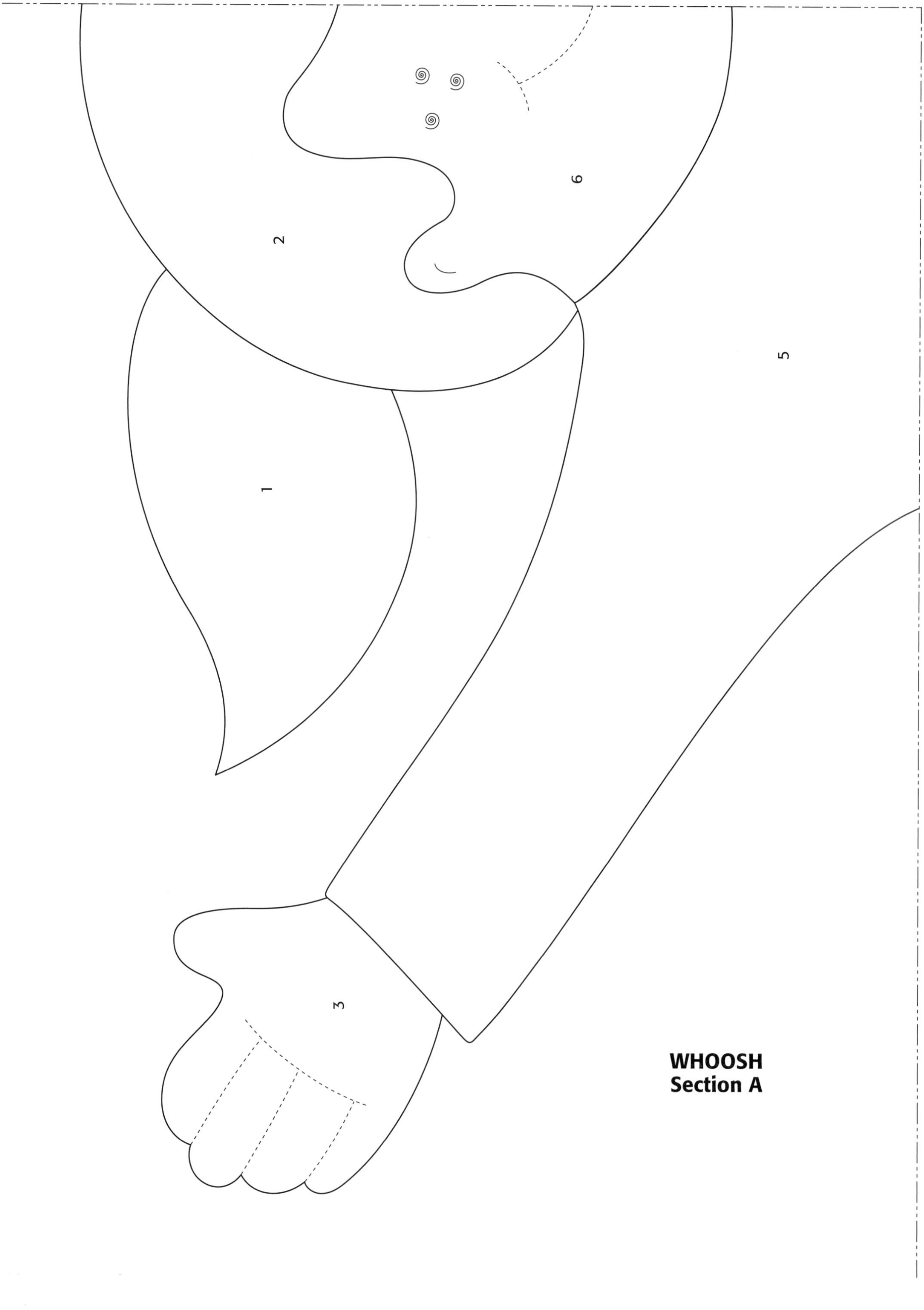

74

2

6

5

1

3

**WHOOSH
Section A**

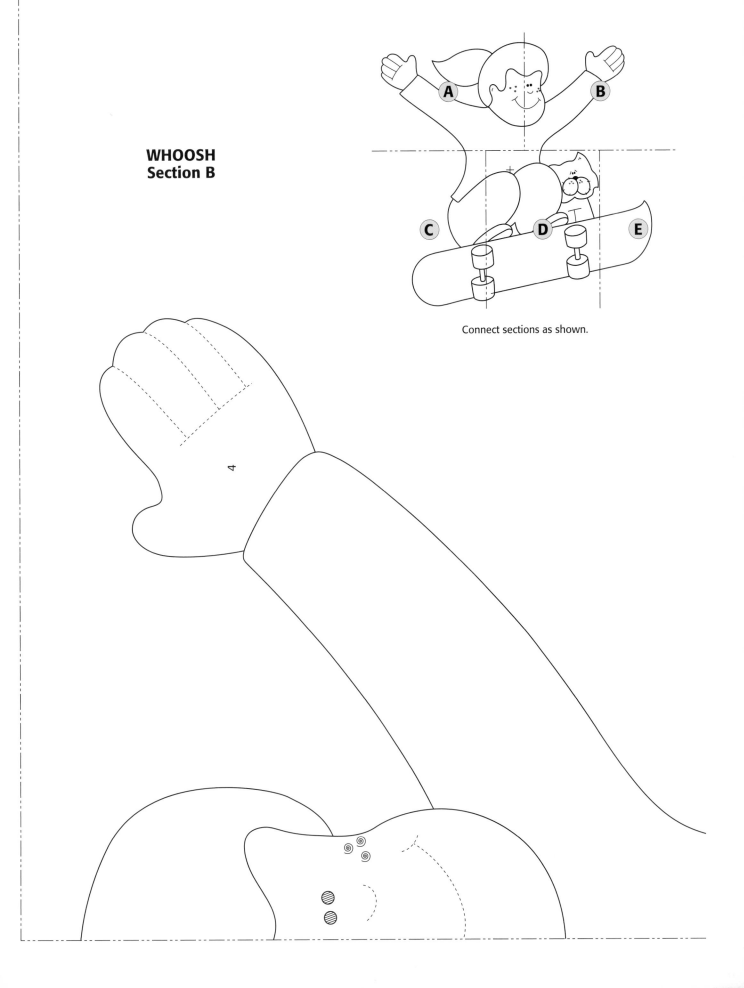

**WHOOSH
Section B**

Connect sections as shown.

A B C D E

4

WHOOSH
Section C

12

22

21

20

19

18

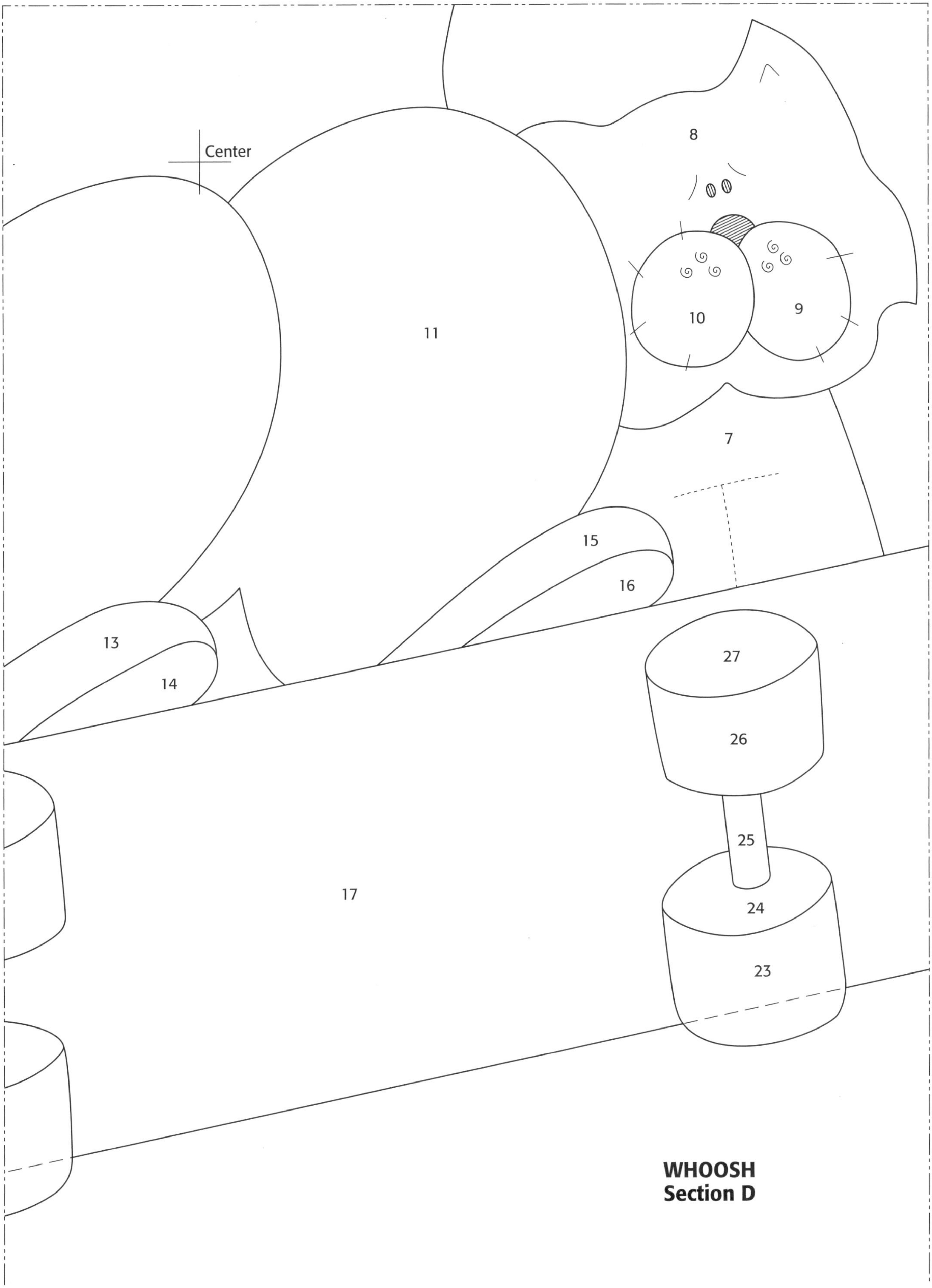

Center

8

10   9

7

11

15

16

13

14

27

26

25

24

23

17

WHOOSH
Section D

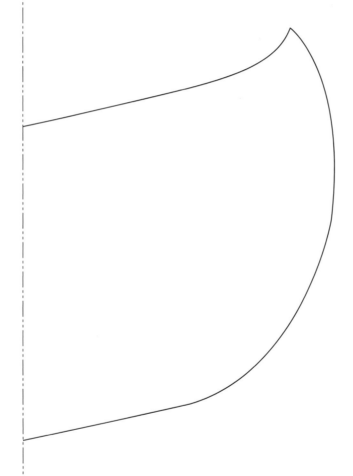

WHOOSH
Section E

About the Author

Although Barbara Roberts discovered quilting in 1979, her interest in it didn't blossom until she took her first appliqué class with Mimi Dietrich in the 1980s. Her previous book for Martingale & Company, *Decoupage Quilts* (1995), involved fusible-web appliqué and was inspired by her love for appliqué.

From 1993 to 1999, Barbara ran her own pattern business, Hannily Patterns. She created over 60 patterns for projects such as quilts, dolls, and crafts. Today her interests include appliqué, miniature tapestry weaving, miniature woven dolls, doll making, decorative painting, and writing poetry. For the past several years, she has been teaching doll making. Three years ago she started a doll group called Dollmakers Anonymous in her hometown. Barbara lives in Catonsville, Maryland, with her husband, Jim; two daughters, Emily and Hanna; and two Maltese pups, Sparky and Toby.

Martingale & Company
Toll-free: 1-800-426-3126

International: 1-425-483-3313
24-Hour Fax: 1-425-486-7596

PO Box 118, Bothell, WA 98041-0118 USA

Web site: www.patchwork.com
E-mail: info@martingale-pub.com

Books from

These books are available through your local quilt, fabric, craft-supply, or art-supply store. For more information, contact us for a free full-color catalog. You can also find our full catalog of books online at www.patchwork.com.

Appliqué

Appliqué for Baby
Appliqué in Bloom
Baltimore Bouquets
Basic Quiltmaking Techniques for Hand Appliqué
Basic Quiltmaking Techniques for Machine Appliqué
Coxcomb Quilt
The Easy Art of Appliqué
Folk Art Animals
Fun with Sunbonnet Sue
Garden Appliqué
The Nursery Rhyme Quilt
Red and Green: An Appliqué Tradition
Rose Sampler Supreme
Stars in the Garden
Sunbonnet Sue All Through the Year

Beginning Quiltmaking

Basic Quiltmaking Techniques for Borders & Bindings
Basic Quiltmaking Techniques for Curved Piecing
Basic Quiltmaking Techniques for Divided Circles
Basic Quiltmaking Techniques for Eight-Pointed Stars
Basic Quiltmaking Techniques for Hand Appliqué
Basic Quiltmaking Techniques for Machine Appliqué
Basic Quiltmaking Techniques for Strip Piecing
The Quilter's Handbook
Your First Quilt Book (or it should be!)

Crafts

15 Beads
Fabric Mosaics
Folded Fabric Fun
Making Memories

Cross-Stitch & Embroidery

Hand-Stitched Samplers from I Done My Best
Kitties to Stitch and Quilt: 15 Redwork Designs
Miniature Baltimore Album Quilts
A Silk-Ribbon Album

Designing Quilts

Color: The Quilter's Guide
Design Essentials: The Quilter's Guide
Design Your Own Quilts
Designing Quilts: The Value of Value
The Nature of Design
QuiltSkills
Sensational Settings
Surprising Designs from Traditional Quilt Blocks
Whimsies & Whynots

Holiday

Christmas Ribbonry
Easy Seasonal Wall Quilts
Favorite Christmas Quilts from That Patchwork Place
Holiday Happenings
Quilted for Christmas
Quilted for Christmas, Book IV
Special-Occasion Table Runners
Welcome to the North Pole

Home Decorating

The Home Decorator's Stamping Book
Make Room for Quilts
Special-Occasion Table Runners
Stitch & Stencil
Welcome Home: Debbie Mumm
Welcome Home: Kaffe Fassett

Knitting

Simply Beautiful Sweaters
Two Sticks and a String

Paper Arts

The Art of Handmade Paper and Collage
Grow Your Own Paper
Stamp with Style

Paper Piecing

Classic Quilts with Precise Foundation Piecing
Easy Machine Paper Piecing
Easy Mix & Match Machine Paper Piecing
Easy Paper-Pieced Keepsake Quilts
Easy Paper-Pieced Miniatures
Easy Reversible Vests
Go Wild with Quilts
Go Wild with Quilts—Again!
It's Raining Cats & Dogs
Mariner's Medallion
Needles and Notions
Paper-Pieced Curves
Paper Piecing the Seasons
A Quilter's Ark
Sewing on the Line
Show Me How to Paper Piece

Quilting & Finishing Techniques

The Border Workbook
Borders by Design
A Fine Finish
Happy Endings
Interlacing Borders
Lap Quilting Lives!
Loving Stitches
Machine Quilting Made Easy
Quilt It!
Quilting Design Sourcebook
Quilting Makes the Quilt
The Ultimate Book of Quilt Labels

Ribbonry

Christmas Ribbonry
A Passion for Ribbonry
Wedding Ribbonry

Rotary Cutting & Speed Piecing

101 Fabulous Rotary-Cut Quilts
365 Quilt Blocks a Year Perpetual Calendar
All-Star Sampler
Around the Block with Judy Hopkins
Basic Quiltmaking Techniques for Strip Piecing
Beyond Log Cabin
Block by Block
Easy Stash Quilts
Fat Quarter Quilts
The Joy of Quilting
A New Twist on Triangles
A Perfect Match
Quilters on the Go
ScrapMania
Shortcuts
Simply Scrappy Quilts
Spectacular Scraps
Square Dance
Stripples Strikes Again!
Strips That Sizzle
Surprising Designs from Traditional Quilt Blocks

Traditional Quilts with Painless Borders
Time-Crunch Quilts
Two-Color Quilts

Small & Miniature Quilts

Bunnies by the Bay Meets Little Quilts
Celebrate! With Little Quilts
Easy Paper-Pieced Miniatures
Fun with Miniature Log Cabin Blocks
Little Quilts all Through the House
Living with Little Quilts
Miniature Baltimore Album Quilts
A Silk-Ribbon Album
Small Quilts Made Easy
Small Wonders

Surface Design

Complex Cloth
Creative Marbling on Fabric
Dyes & Paints
Fantasy Fabrics
Hand-Dyed Fabric Made Easy
Jazz It Up
Machine Quilting with Decorative Threads
New Directions in Chenille
Thread Magic
Threadplay with Libby Lehman

Topics in Quiltmaking

Bargello Quilts
The Cat's Meow
Even More Quilts for Baby
Everyday Angels in Extraordinary Quilts
Fabric Collage Quilts
Fast-and-Fun Stenciled Quilts
Folk Art Quilts
It's Raining Cats & Dogs
Kitties to Stitch and Quilt: 15 Redwork Designs
Life in the Country with Country Threads
Machine-Stitched Cathedral Windows
More Quilts for Baby
A New Slant on Bargello Quilts
Patchwork Pantry
Pink Ribbon Quilts
Quilted Landscapes
The Quilted Nursery
Quilting Your Memories
Quilts for Baby
Quilts from Aunt Amy
Whimsies & Whynots

Watercolor Quilts

More Strip-Pieced Watercolor Magic
Quick Watercolor Quilts
Strip-Pieced Watercolor Magic
Watercolor Impressions
Watercolor Quilts

Wearables

Easy Reversible Vests
Just Like Mommy
New Directions in Chenille
Quick-Sew Fleece
Variations in Chenille